Ottawa Ontario Book 3 in Colour Photos, Saving Our History One Photo at a Time

Photography by Barbara Raué 2016

Series Name: Cruising Ontario

Book 148: Ottawa Book 3

Cover photo: 197 Wurtemburg Street, Page 53

Series Name: Cruising Ontario
Saving Our History One Photo at a Time
in colour photos

Books Available in Alphabetical Order:
Aberfoyle, Acton, Alton, Amherstburg, Ancaster, Arthur, Aylmer, Ayr, Bloomingdale, Brantford, Burlington, Caledon, Caledonia, Cambridge, Clifford, Conestogo, Delhi, Dorchester to Aylmer, Drayton, Drumbo, Dundas, Eden Mills, Elmira, Elora, Essex, Fergus, Guelph, Hagersville, Hamilton, Hanover, Harriston, Hespeler, Jarvis, Kingston, Kingsville, Kitchener, Linwood, Listowel, London, Lucknow, Mono, Mount Forest, Neustadt, New Hamburg, Niagara-on-the-Lake, Oakville, Orangeville, Orillia, Owen Sound, Palmerston, Peterborough, Petrolia, Port Elgin, Preston, Rockwood, Sarnia, Seaforth, Sheffield, Shelburne, Simcoe, Southampton, St. Jacobs, St. Marys, St. Thomas, Stoney Creek, Stratford, Thamesford, Tillsonburg, Waterdown, Waterford, Waterloo, Welland, Wellesley, Windsor, Wingham, Woodstock

Other Books by Barbara Raue

Coins of Gold

Arrows, Indians and Love

The Life and Times of Barbara
Volume 1: Inventions That Have Enhanced My Life
Volume 2: Entertainment That I Have Enjoyed
Volume 3: East Coast Trips
Volume 4: Olympics Have Always Intrigued Me
Volume 5: Wonders of the World
Volume 6: Caribbean Cruises We Have Enjoyed
Volume 7: Animals
Volume 8: Storms and Other Major Disasters in My Lifetime
Volume 9: Wars, Terrorist Attacks and Major Disasters

The Cromwell Family Book

Laura Secord Discovered

Daddy Where Are You?

Montana Series
Book 1: Montana Dream
Book 2: Life on the Montana Frontier
Book 3: Montana to Boston and Back

Visit Barbara's website to view all of her books
http://barbararaue.ca

Table of Contents

Rideau Hall

Thomas MacKay, a wealthy Scottish stonemason and entrepreneur, helped build the Rideau Canal. Following the completion of the canal, McKay built mills at Rideau Falls, making him the founder of New Edinburgh, the original settlement of Ottawa. With his newly acquired wealth, McKay purchased the 100 acre site overlooking both the Ottawa and Rideau Rivers and built a stone villa in 1838 where he and his family lived until 1855. The building, an eleven-room mansion, was known as MacKay Castle.

Following Confederation, Rideau Hall was purchased by the Canadian government as a permanent vice regal residence and home for the nation's first governor general, Lord Monck. Subsequent governor generals expanded and improved the original building to carry out their increasing official duties. Lord Dufferin added the wings on either side of the main entrance in the 1870s.

The architecture styles are Late Georgian, Romanesque and Florentine Renaissance Revival. One of the greatest alterations to the form of Rideau Hall came in 1913 when the Duke of Connaught had the new main entrance installed with its carved Royal Coat of Arms in an adapted Florentine architectural style. The block is three stories in height, and its front is divided by pilasters into five bays, with the central one slightly wider than the equal other four. The windows on the main floor are each surrounded by smaller pilasters beneath a triangular pediment, while the second level windows are each simply framed by a half-round molding surrounded by two flat planes broken at the top by a keystone. A heavy entablature separates the second and third levels, which has less pronounced pilasters and simply framed windows, with the entire facade capped by a narrow cornice and a pediment with a tympanum with the Royal Arms of the United Kingdom.

Rideau Hall stands on an eighty-eight acre estate with the main building consisting of approximately 175 rooms totaling more than 100,000 square feet, and there are twenty-seven outbuildings around the grounds.

Most of Rideau Hall is used for state affairs, with only 5,400 square feet of its area dedicated to private living quarters and additional areas serving as the offices of the Canadian Heraldic Authority (which is responsible for the creation and granting of new coats of arms - armorial bearings, flags, and badges for Canadian citizens and corporate bodies), and the principal workplace of the governor general and his or her staff.

Foreign heads of state are officially received at the hall, as well as both incoming and outgoing ambassadors and high commissioners to Canada, and Canadian Crown ministers. Rideau Hall is the location of many Canadian award presentations and investitures, and where prime ministers and other members of the federal Cabinet are sworn in. There are balls, dinners, garden parties, children's parties, and theatrical productions in the ballroom. The largest event held in the ballroom was a fancy dress ball hosted by the Dufferins that took place on the evening of February 23, 1876 with about 1,500 guests attending.

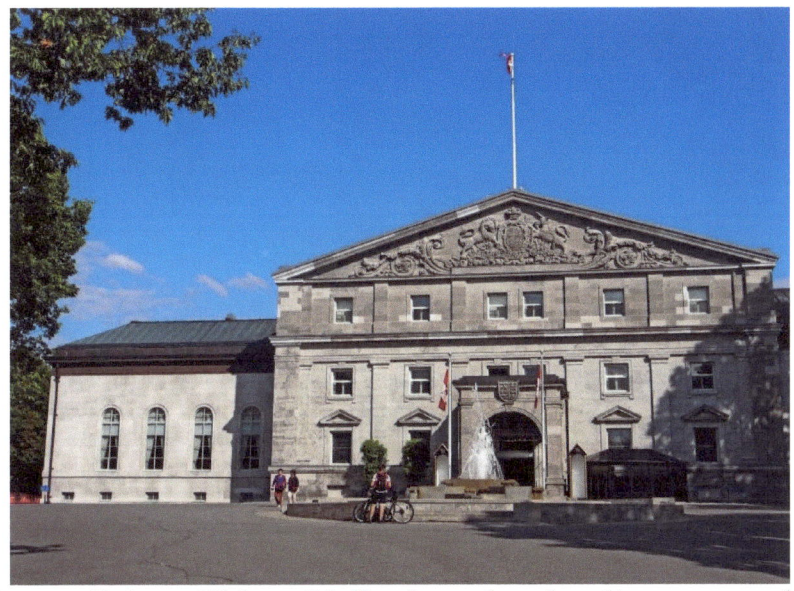

1 Sussex Drive - Rideau Hall – front face has limestone ashlar cladding in an adapted Florentine architectural style, divided by pilasters into five bays

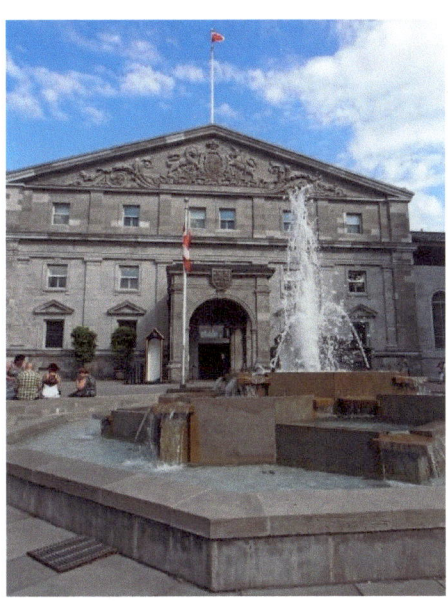

Fountain of Hope built in memory of Terry Fox who raised more than $20 million for Canadian Cancer Research

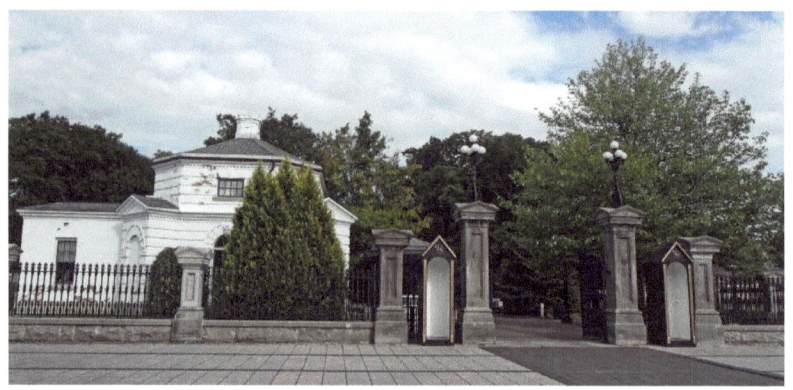

The main gate of Rideau Hall flanked by sentry boxes

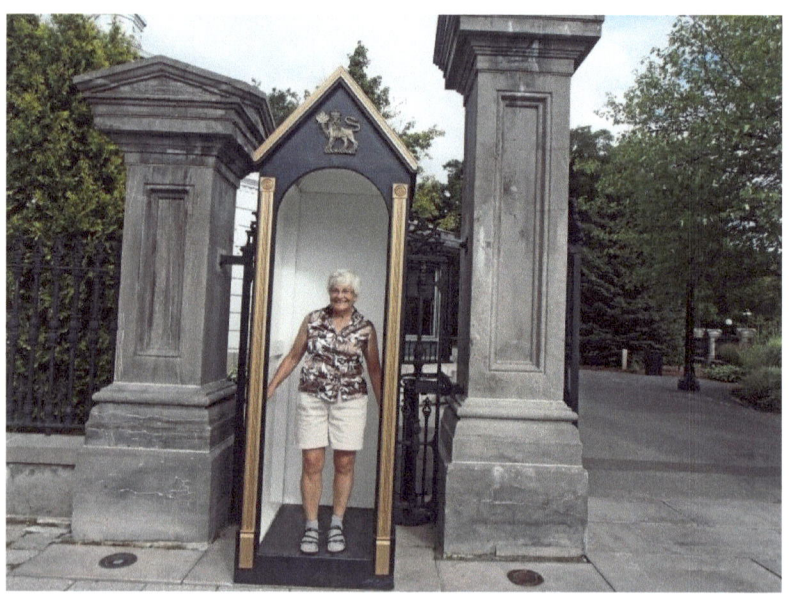

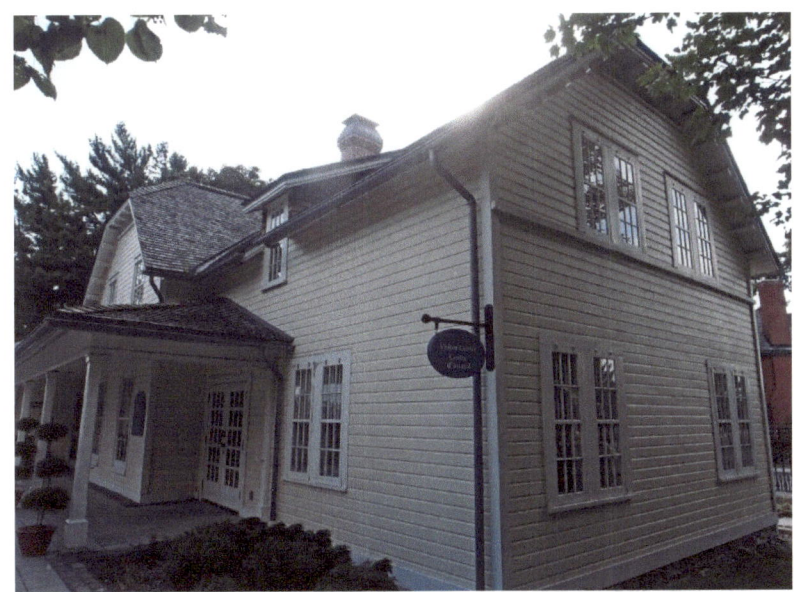

Former Gardener's Cottage, now Visitor Centre

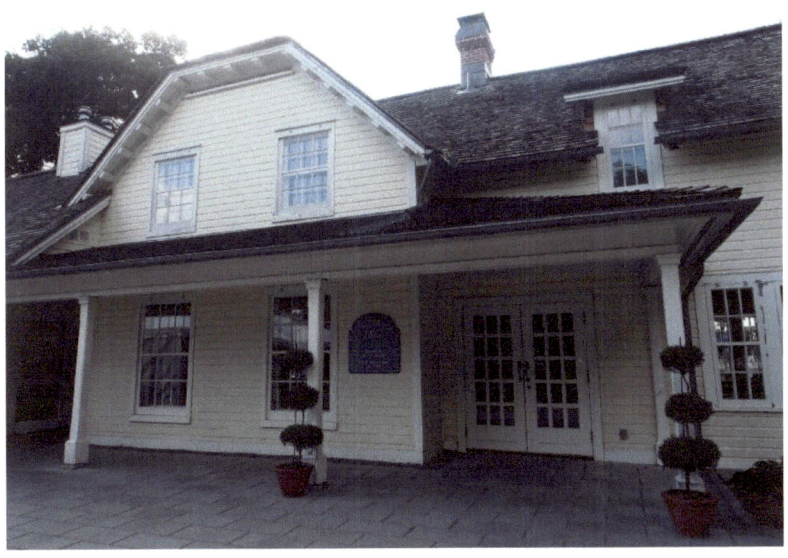

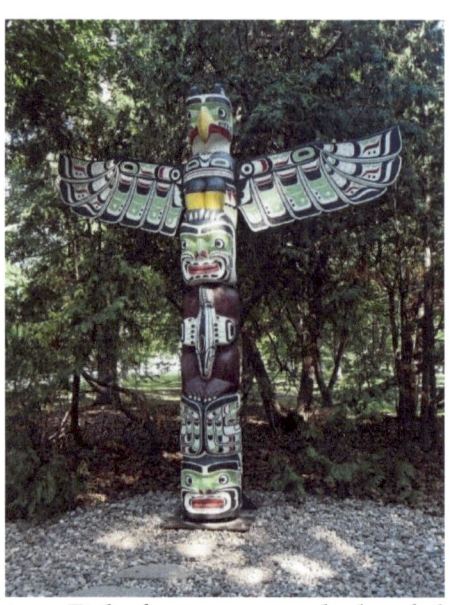

West Coast Totem Pole features symbols of the Pacific coast peoples – topped by a thunderbird, a man holding a salmon, and a double-headed serpent known as sisiutl, one of the most powerful beings in the myths of the people

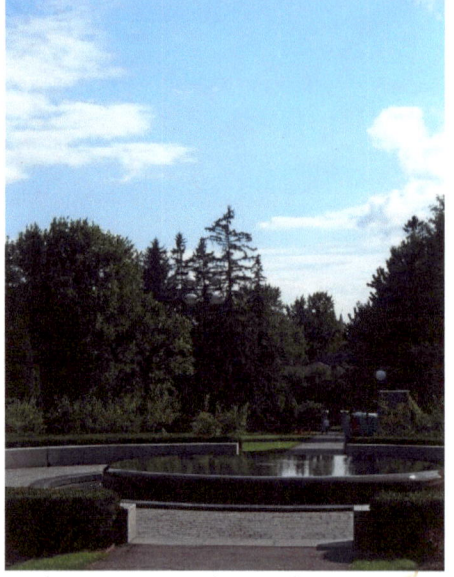

Looking towards Parliament Hill

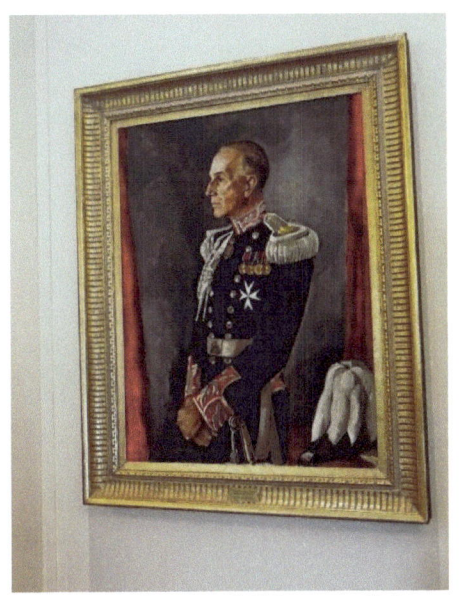

Governor General Vincent Massey

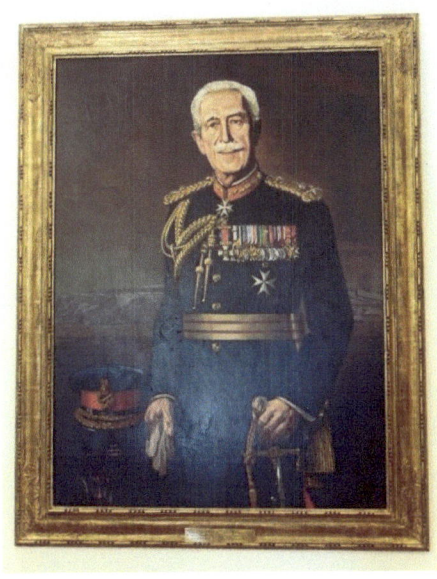

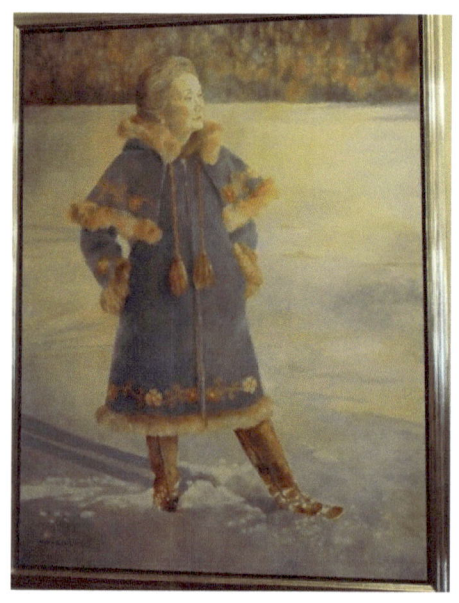

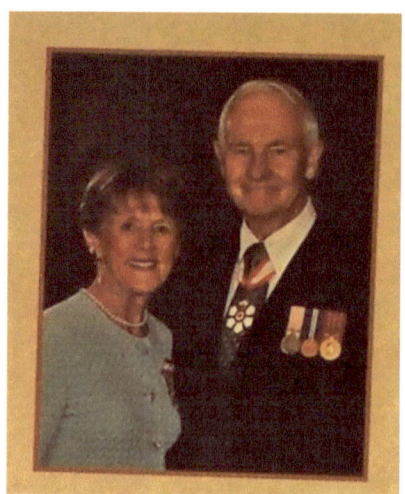

David, Sharon Johnston

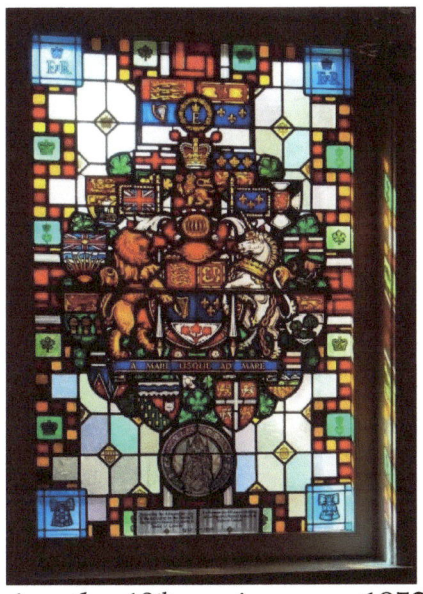

Honoring the 40th anniversary 1952-1992
of Queen Elizabeth II's reign

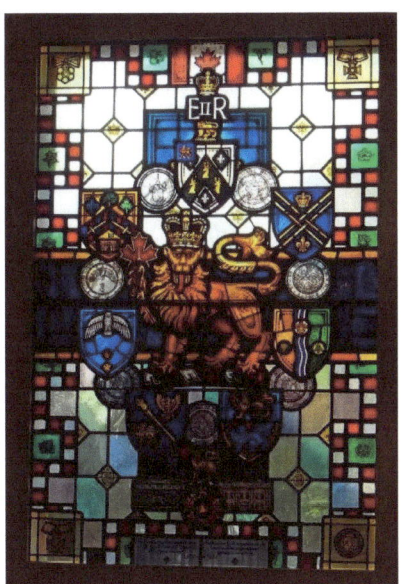

Honoring the 40th anniversary 1952-1992
of appointment of Governor Generals

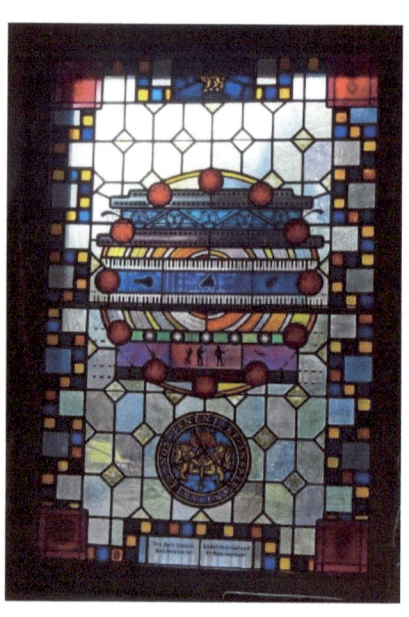

The Arts engage and inspire us

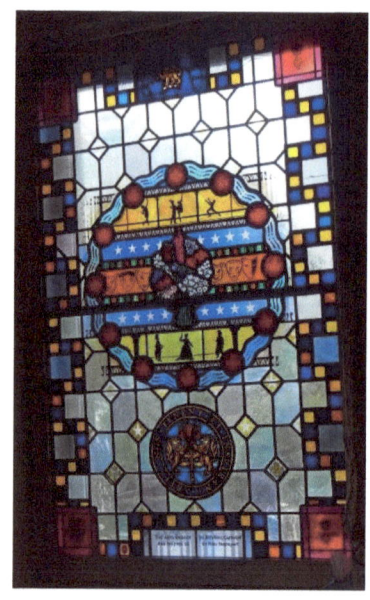

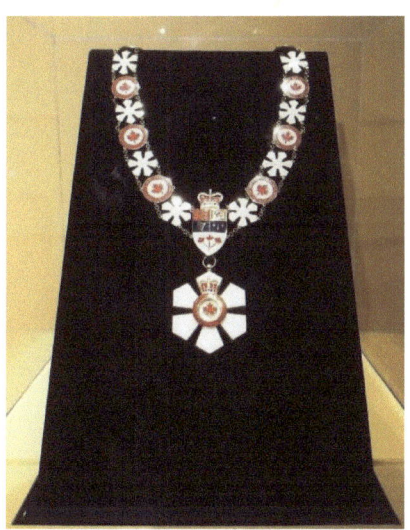

Chancellor's Chain worn by the Governor General during Order of Canada investitures

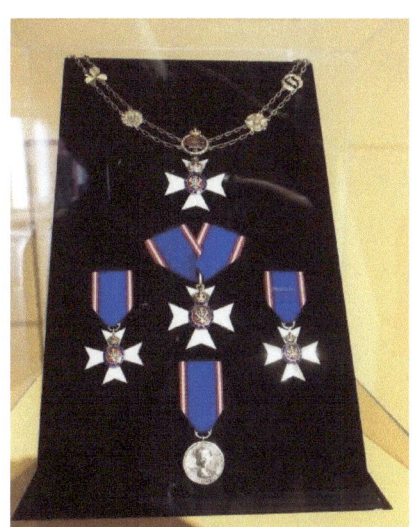

Royal Victorian Chain received by Vincent Massey in 1960, and Roland Michener in 1973

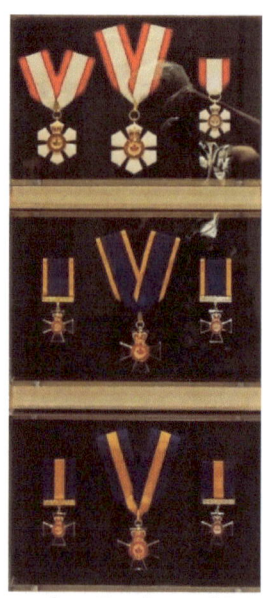

Order of Canada, Order of Military Merit,
Order of Merit of the Police Forces

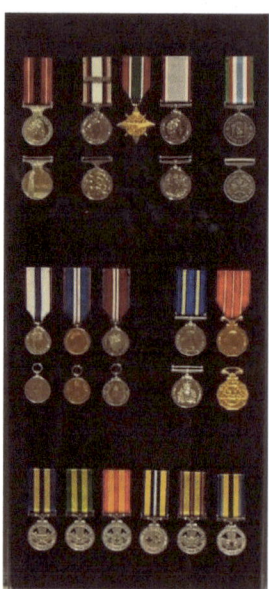

Medals

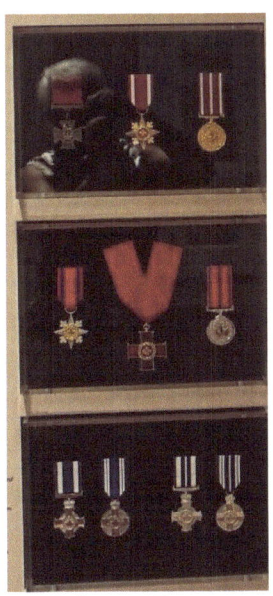

Decorations : Military Valour, Bravery, Meritorious Service

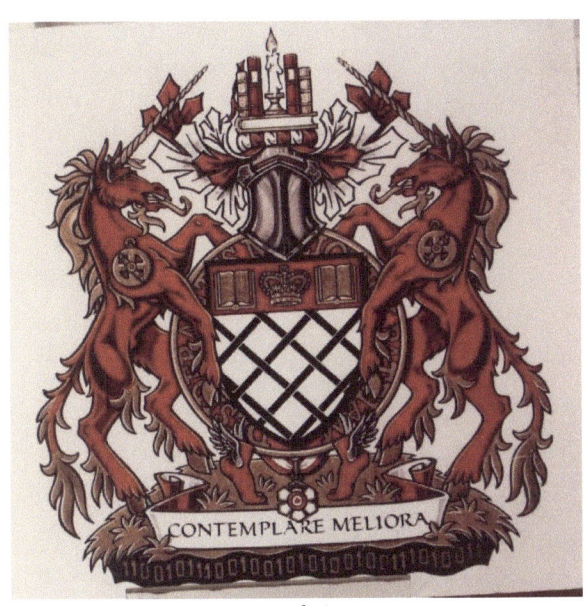

Coat of Arms

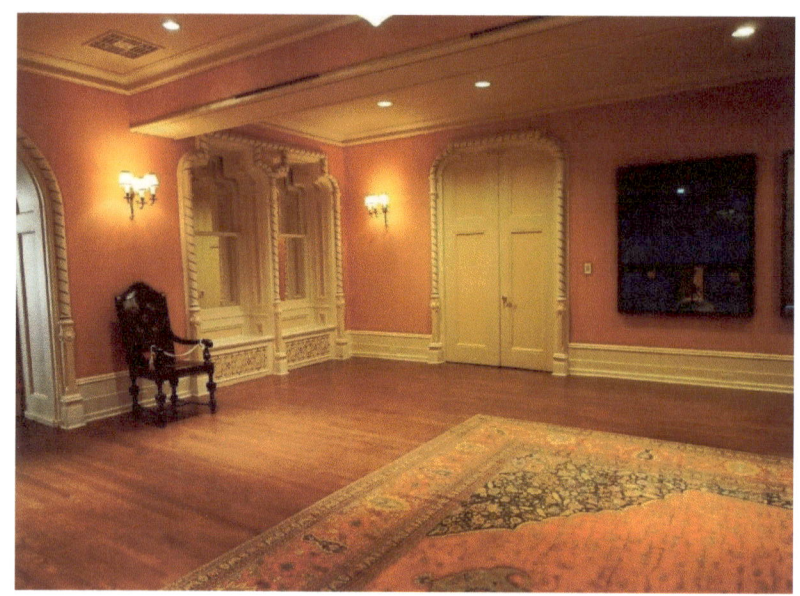

Reception Room

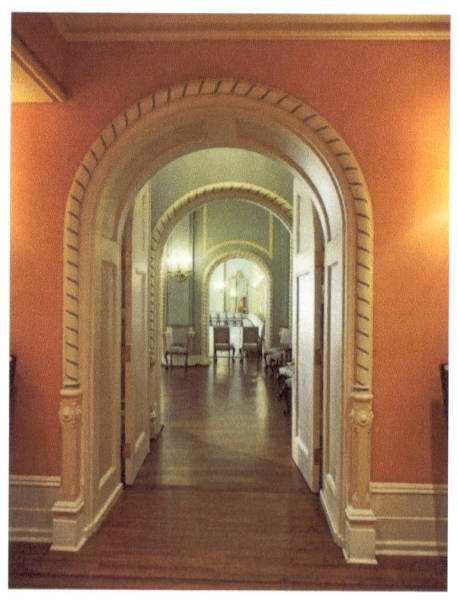

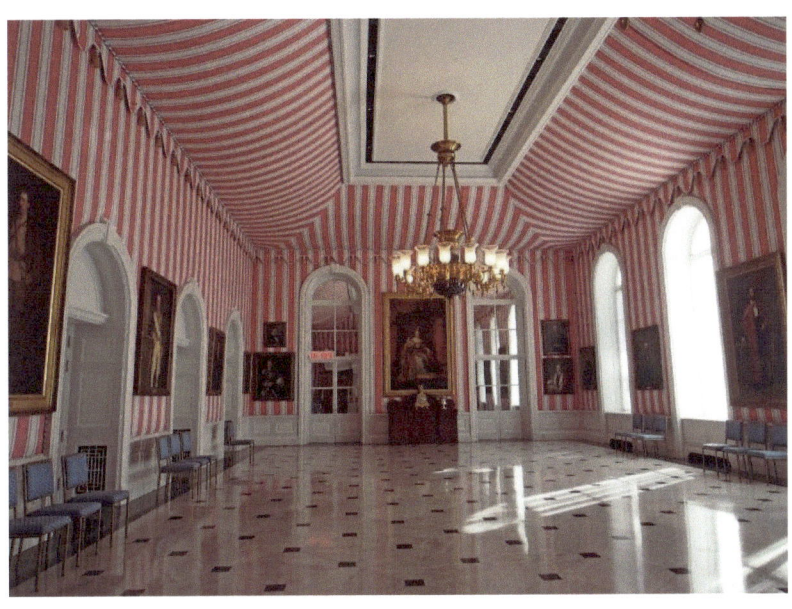

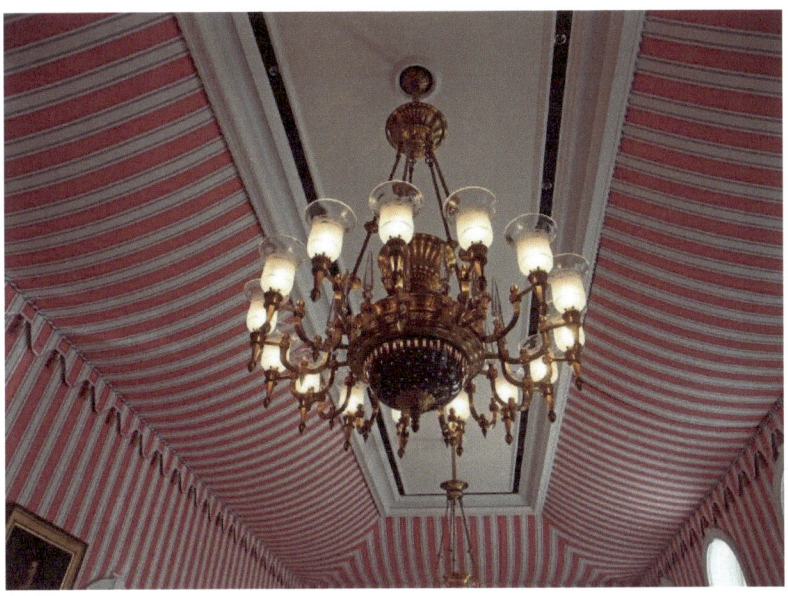

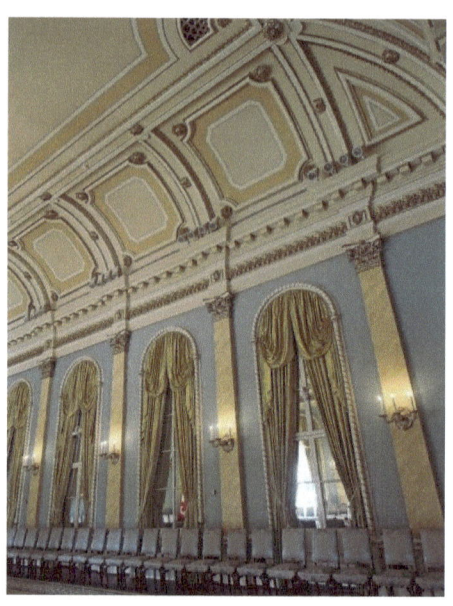

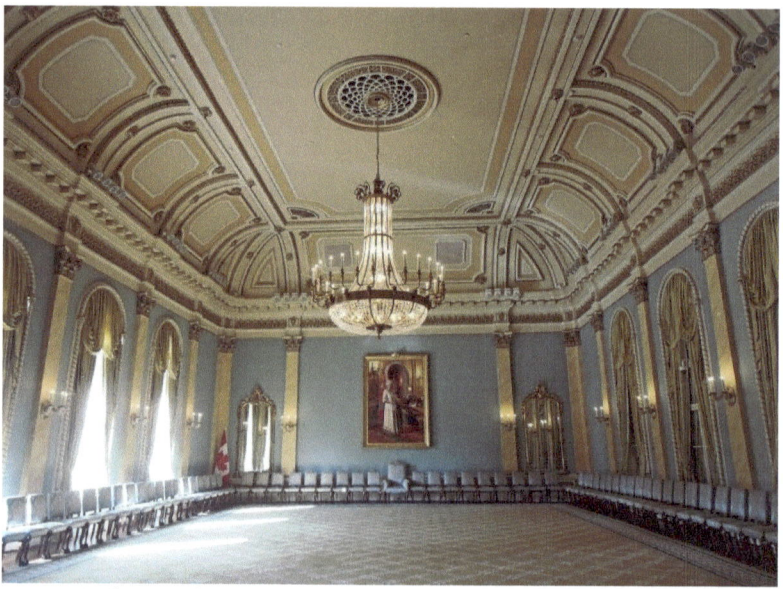

Where dinners are served for heads of state

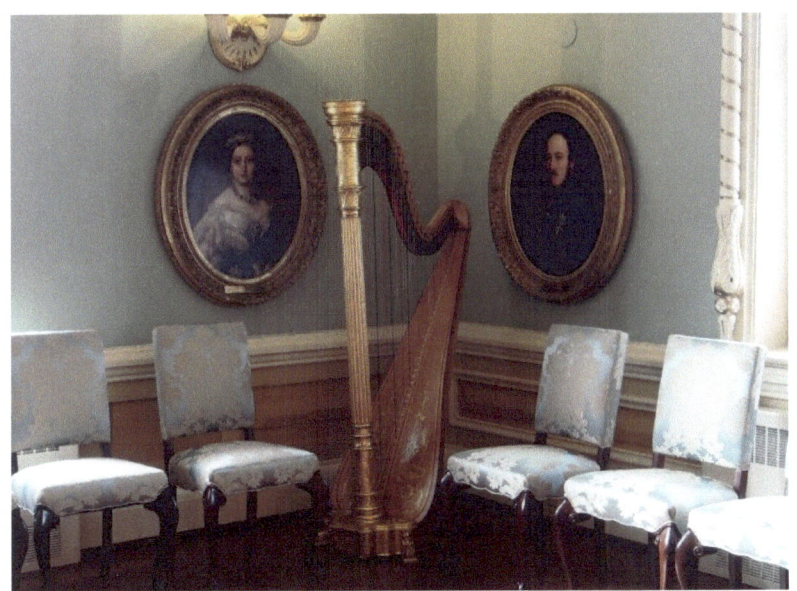

Queen Victoria and Prince Albert

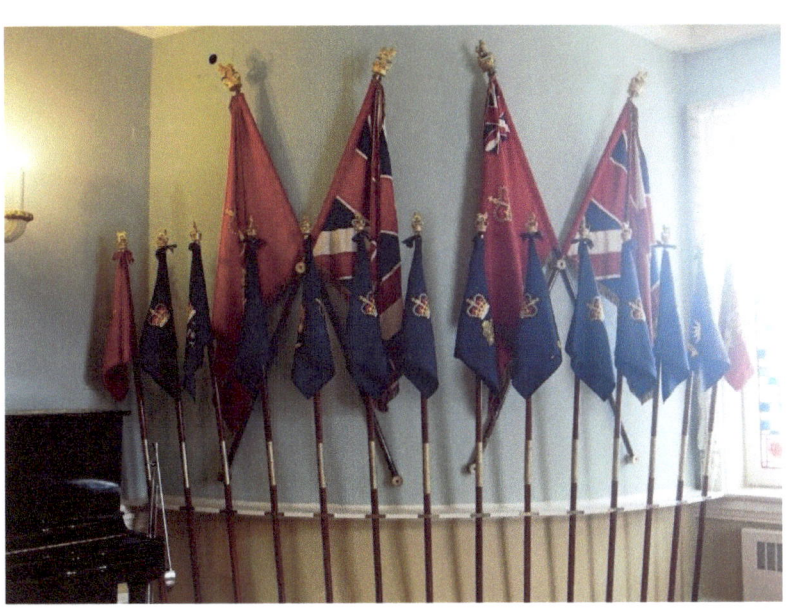

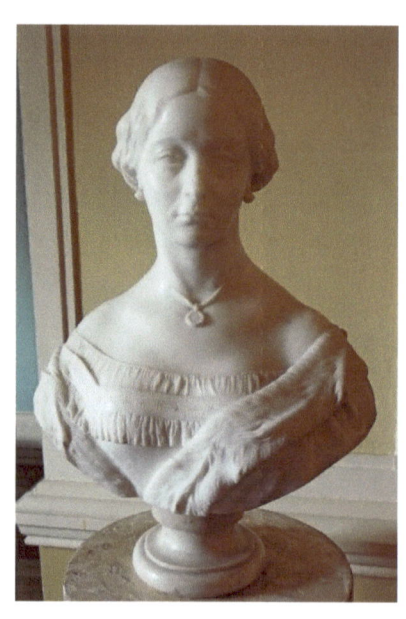

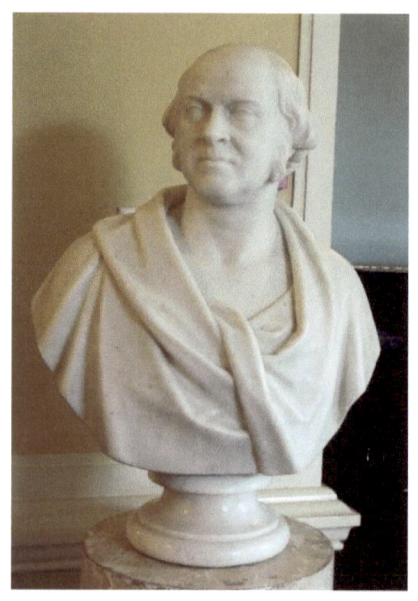

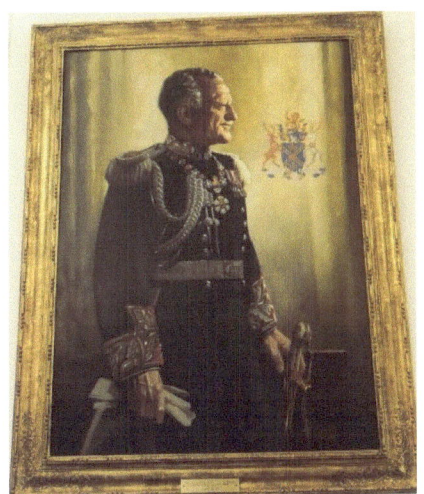

Roland Michener

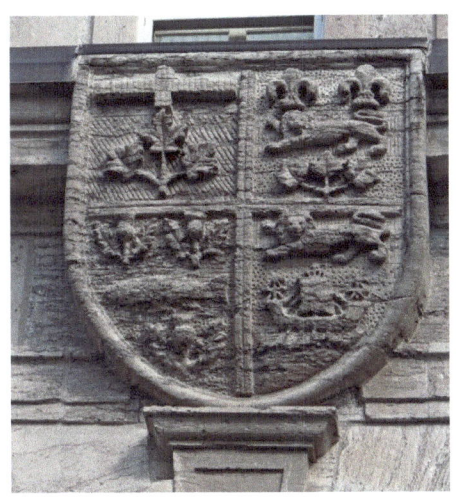

Royal Coat of Arms of the United Kingdom on Rideau Hall
front face

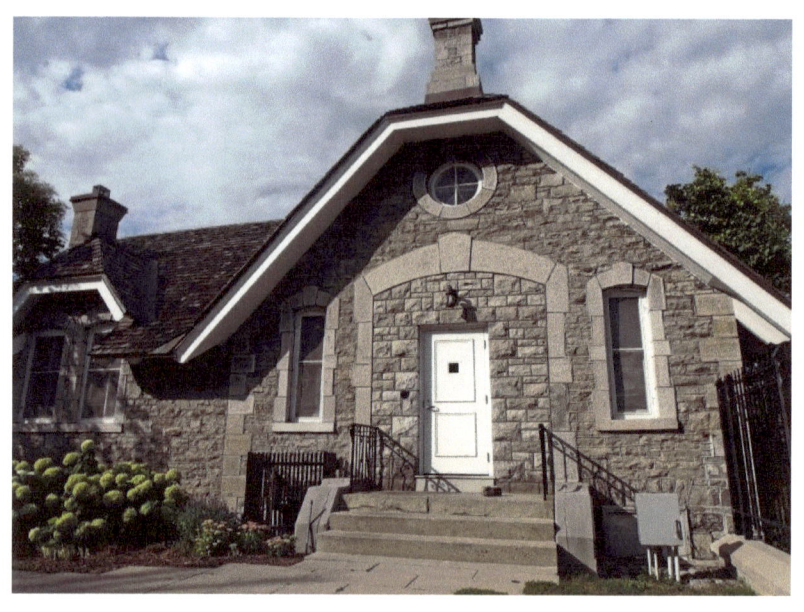

Security structure at entrance to 24 Sussex Drive

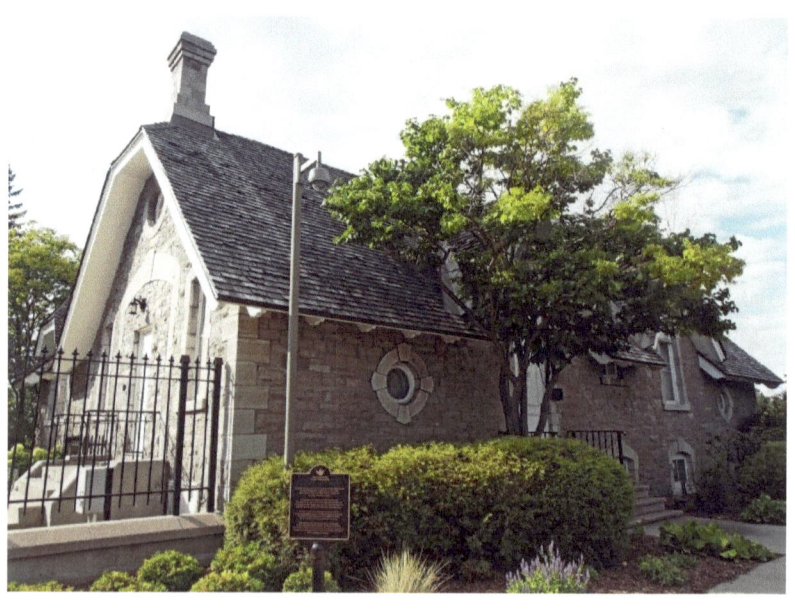

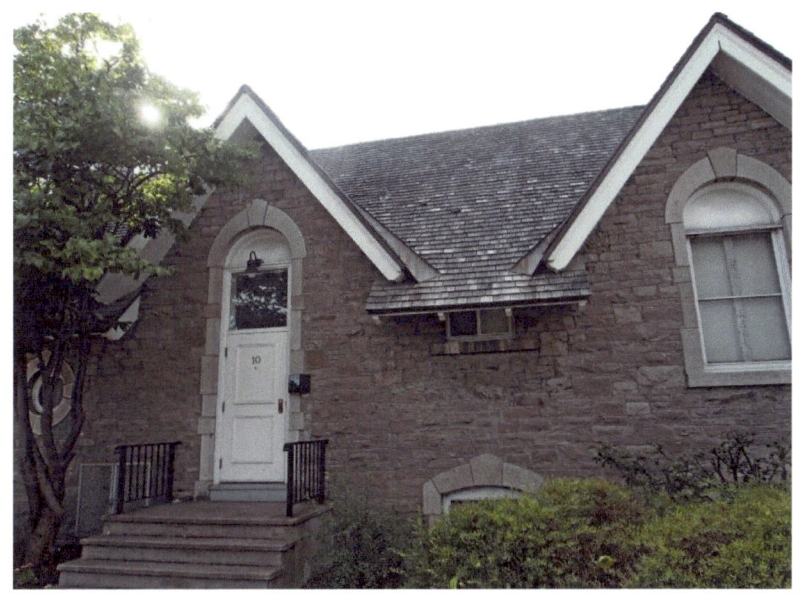

10 Sussex Drive – Gothic – keystones above door and window

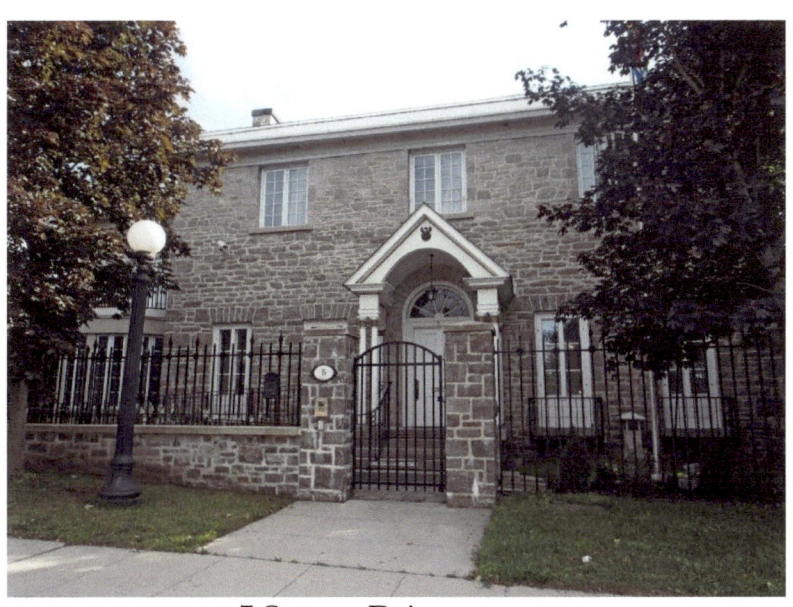

5 Sussex Drive - stone

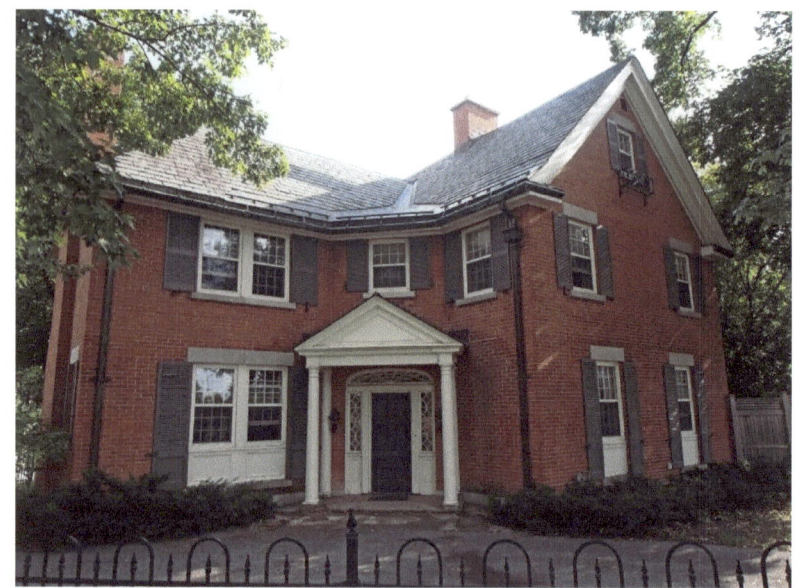

Brick – pediment, sidelights and transom, cornice return on gable

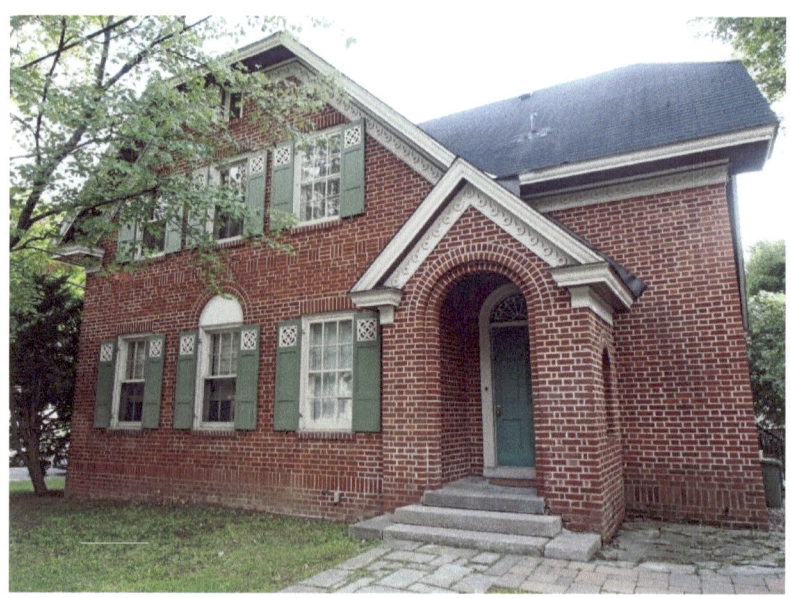

Cornice return on gables - Vernacular

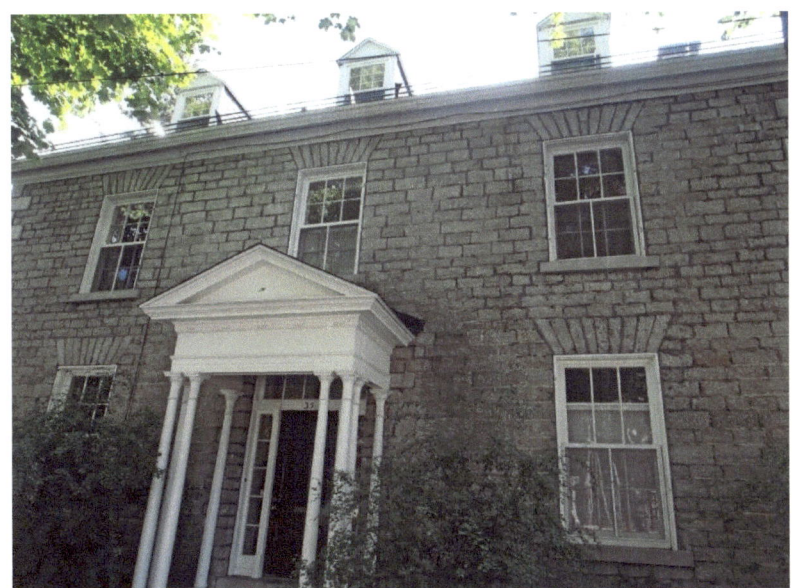

35 Mackay Street – built as a dwelling by James Allen, a tax collector
– 1864-65; it was divided into two dwelling in the 1870s – front door
transoms and sidelights and a formal symmetry characteristic of the
British Classical tradition; Alan Keefer, a local architect, added the
porches in the 1920s

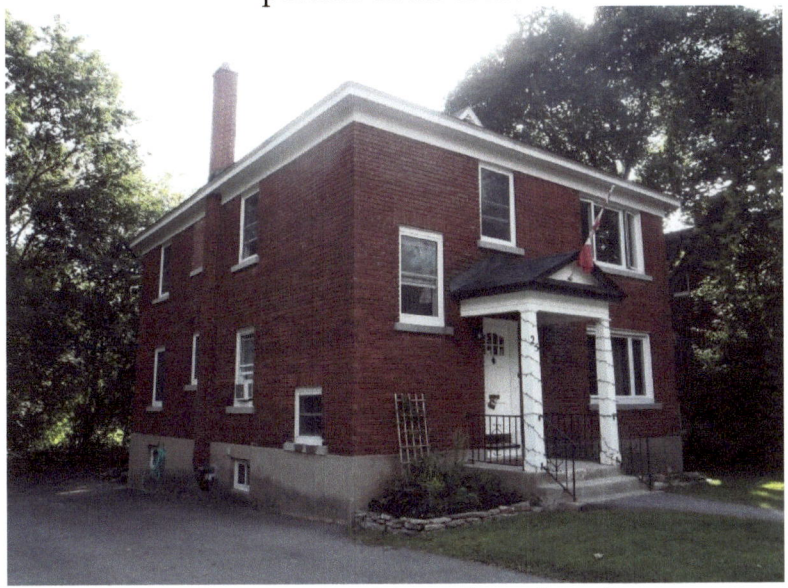

25 Mackay Street – hipped roof, pediment

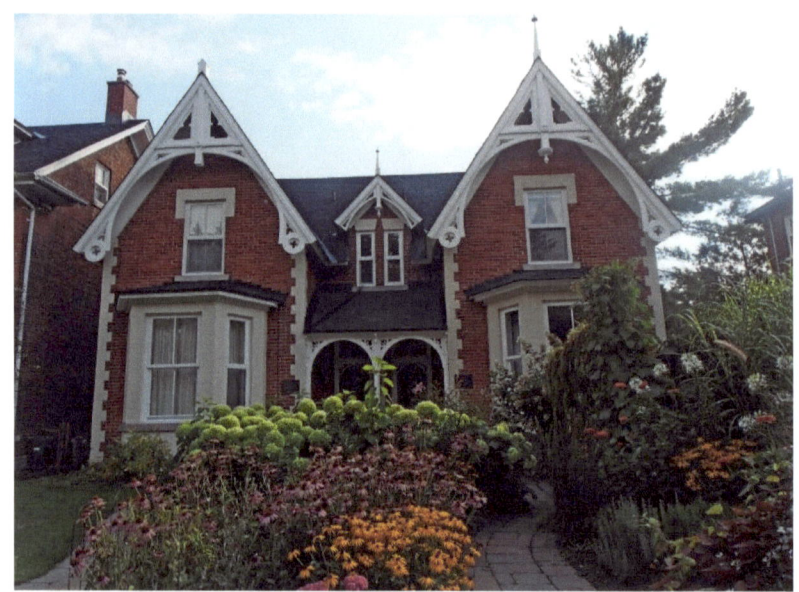

73 Mackay Street – Woodburn House – 1874 – built for William Woodburn, a carpenter – Gothic Revival – verge board trim and finials on gables, corner quoins, bay windows

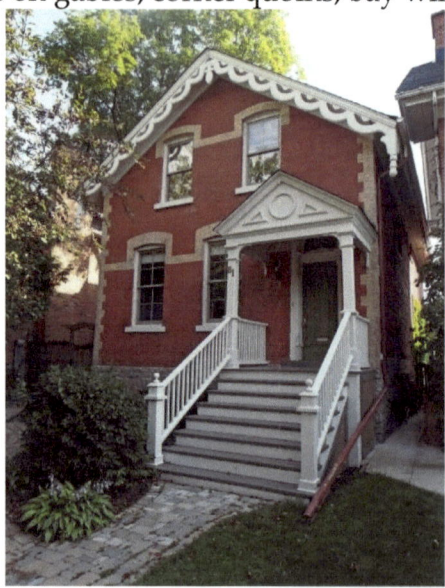

81 Mackay Street – Gothic Revival – verge board trim on gables, banding, corner quoins, pediment with decorative tympanum

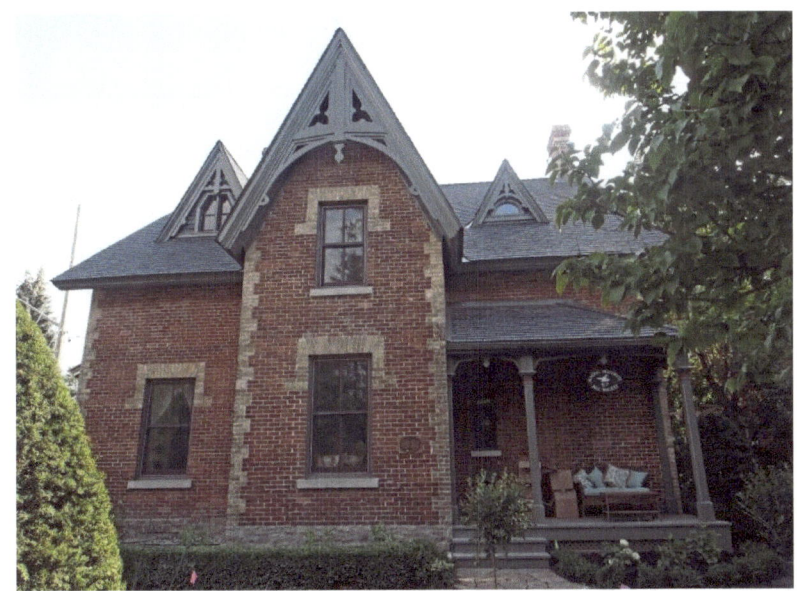

87 Mackay Street – Frechette House – 1877 – Picturesque Gothic style - prominent verge boards, dormers, polychromatic brickwork – occupants Achille and Frechette, chief translator to the House of Commons, and Annie Howells Frechette, a noted writer, held literary evenings here in the 1890s for Ottawa's intellectual elite

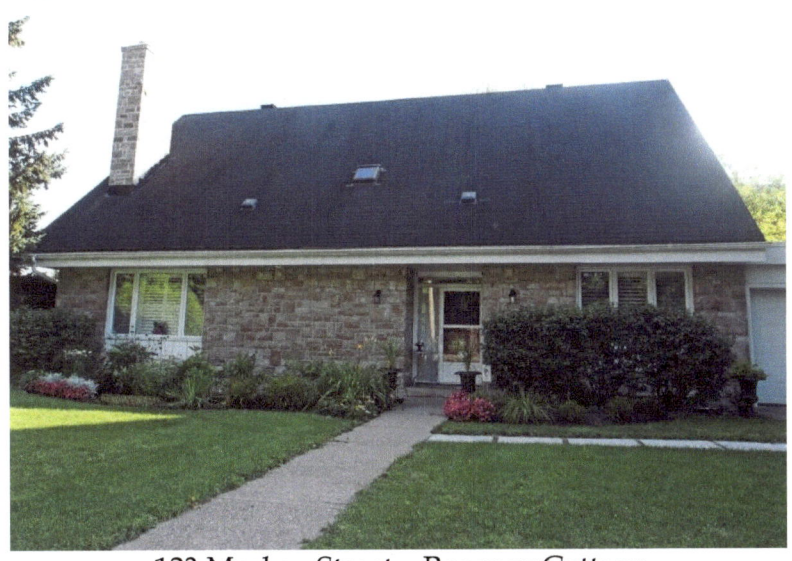

123 Mackay Street – Regency Cottage

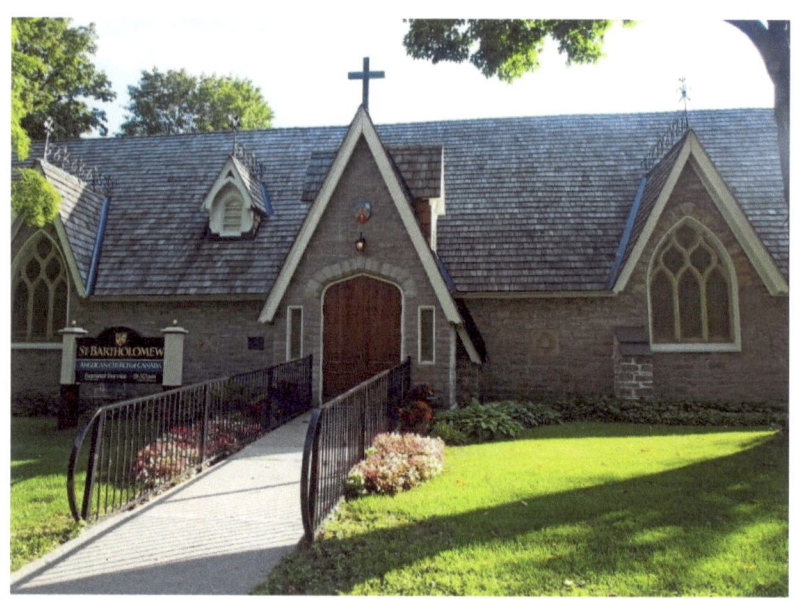

125 Mackay Street (across the street from Rideau Hall) - St. Bartholomew Anglican Church – built in 1868 - A vice-regal pew is reserved for the Governor General at the front of the church. St. Bartholomew's is also the regimental chapel of the Governor General's Foot Guards, and as such has become known as the "Guard's Chapel."

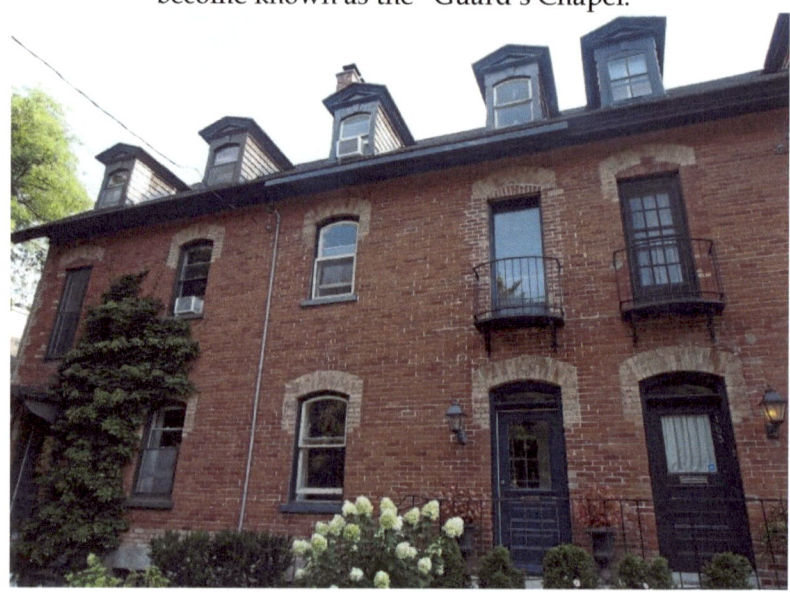

163 Mackay Street – dormers, voussoirs, second-floor balconies

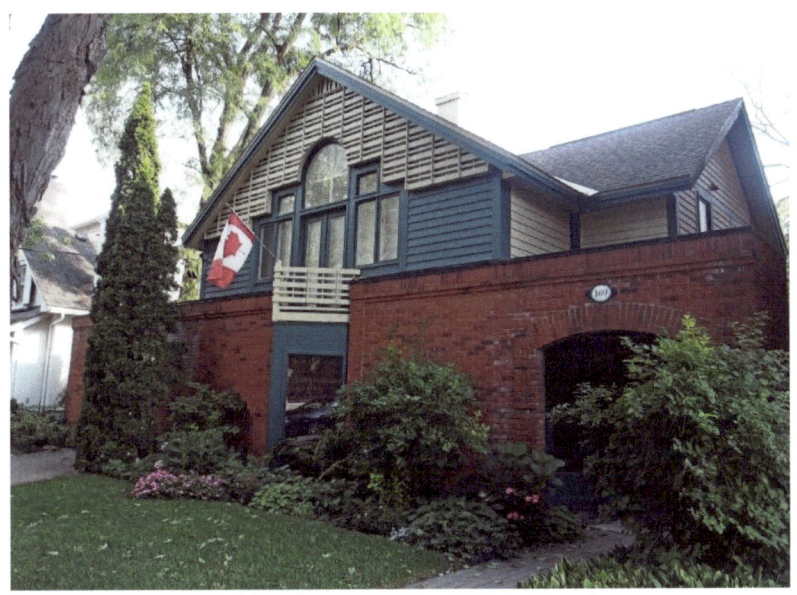

169 Mackay Street - Vernacular

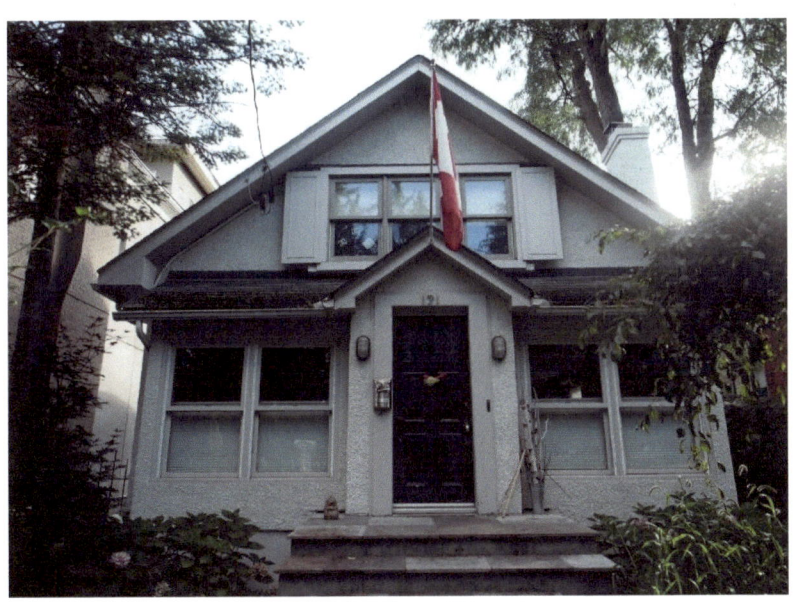

171 Mackay Street

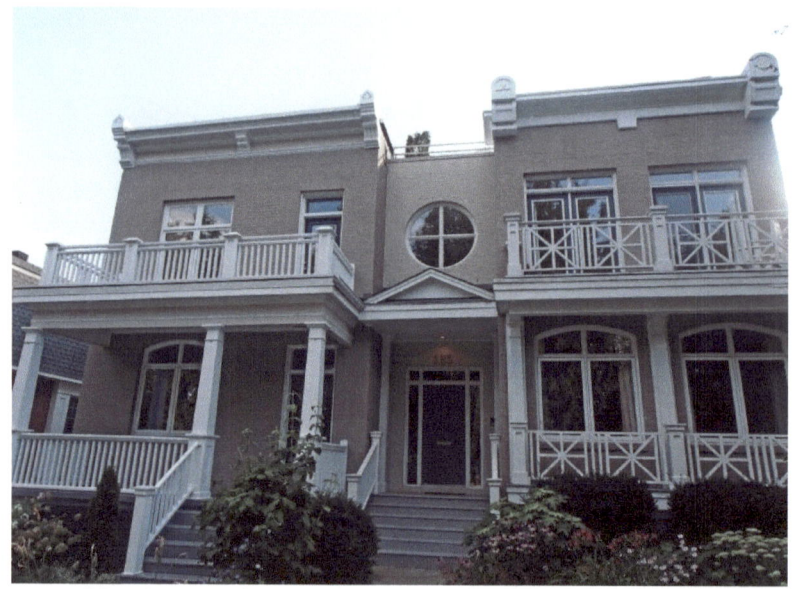

183-185 Mackay Street – second floor balconies

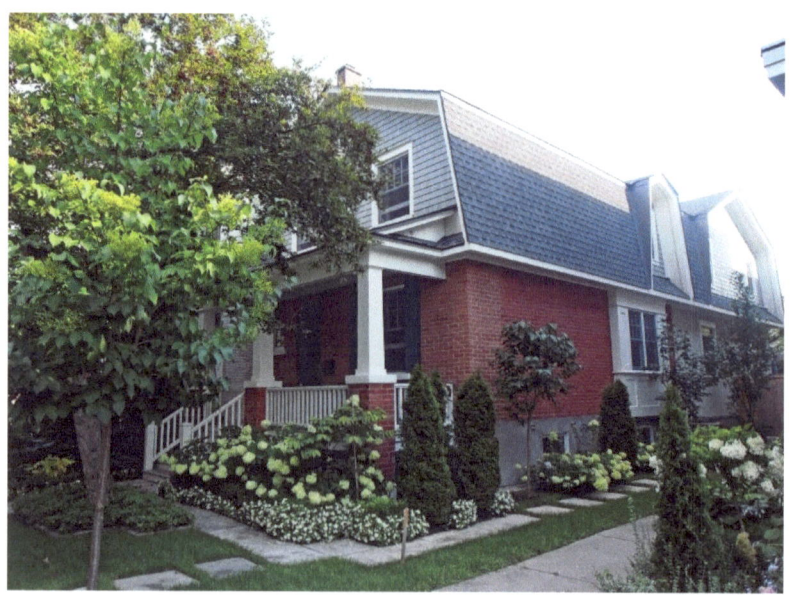

187 Mackay Street – gambrel roof – Neocolonial style

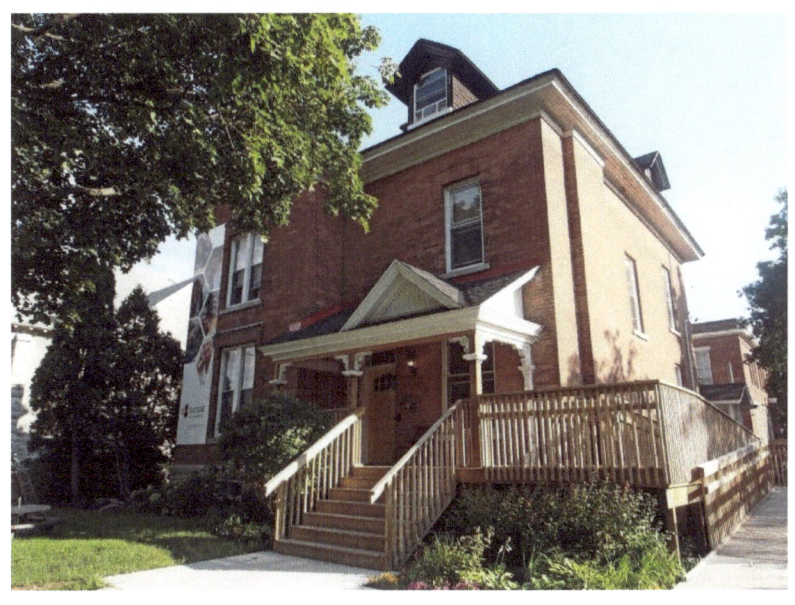

255 Mackay Street – pediment

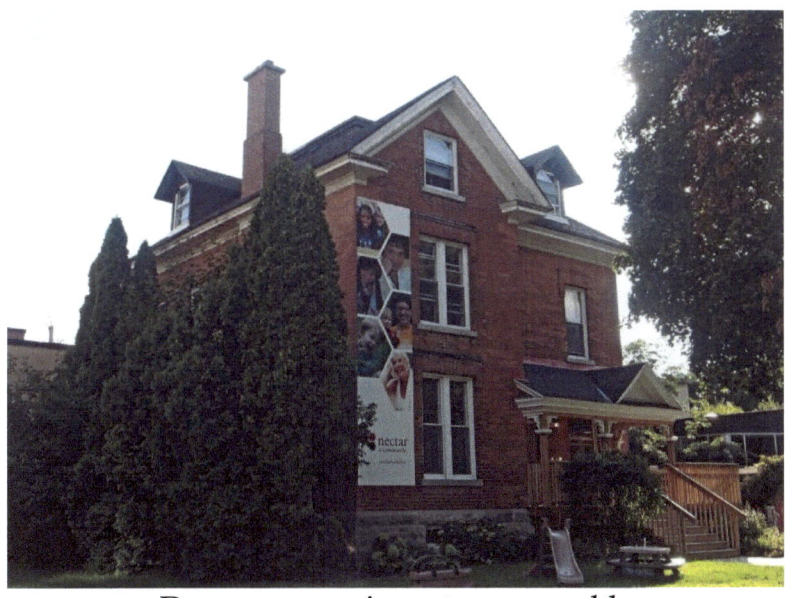

Dormers, cornice return on gable

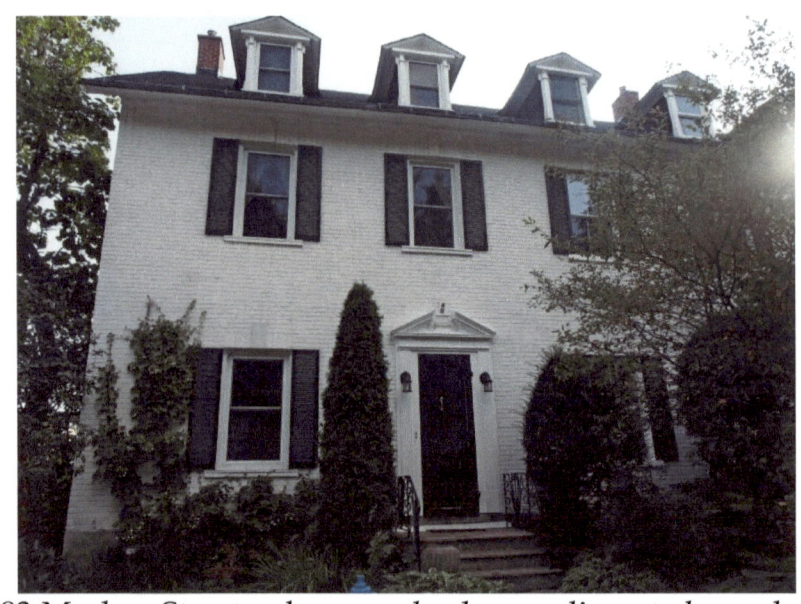

193 Mackay Street – dormers, broken pediment above door
Georgian style

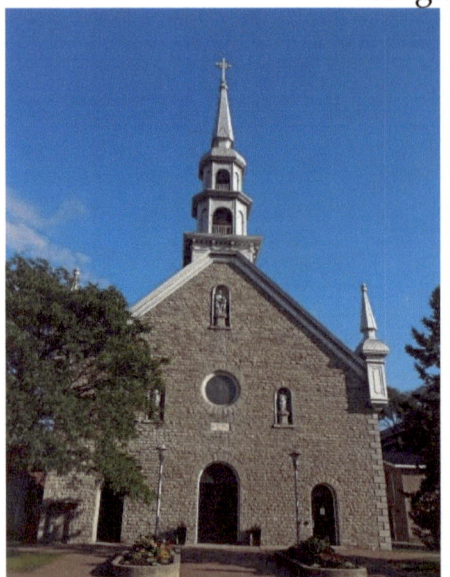 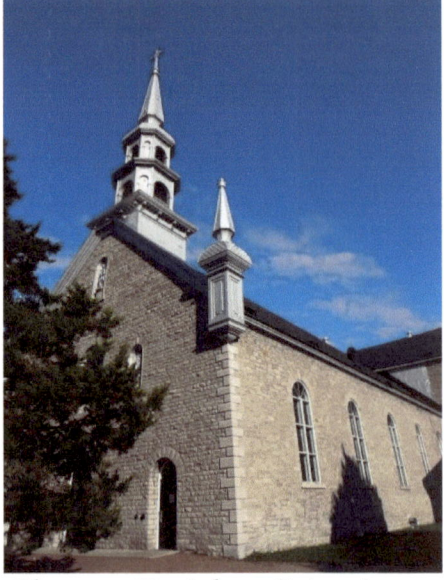

528 Old St. Patrick Street - Saint Clement Parish at Saint Anne
Church – built c. 1880s – Romanesque style – cupola, finials

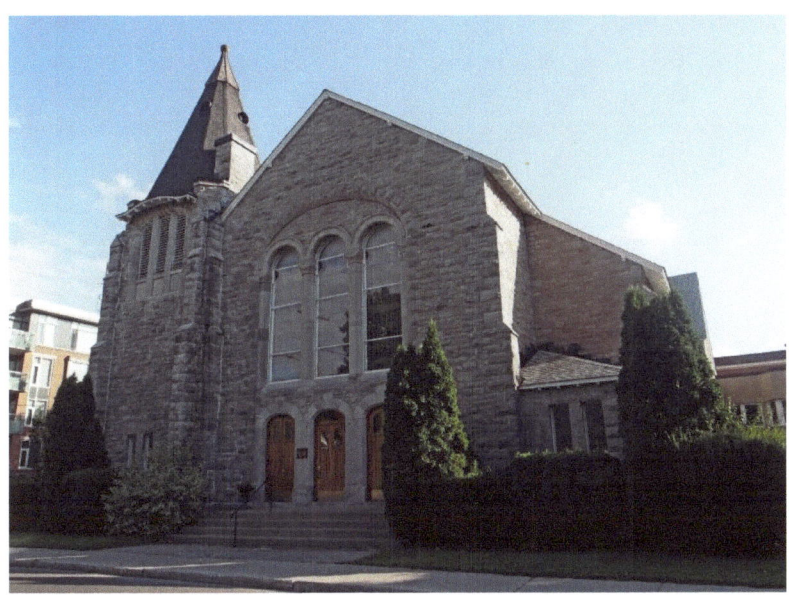

39 Dufferin and Mackay at the southwest corner of the Rideau Hall estate - Mackay United Church – built 1909-1910 – Romanesque Revival architecture – triple-arched entrance portal, round-headed windows, buttresses

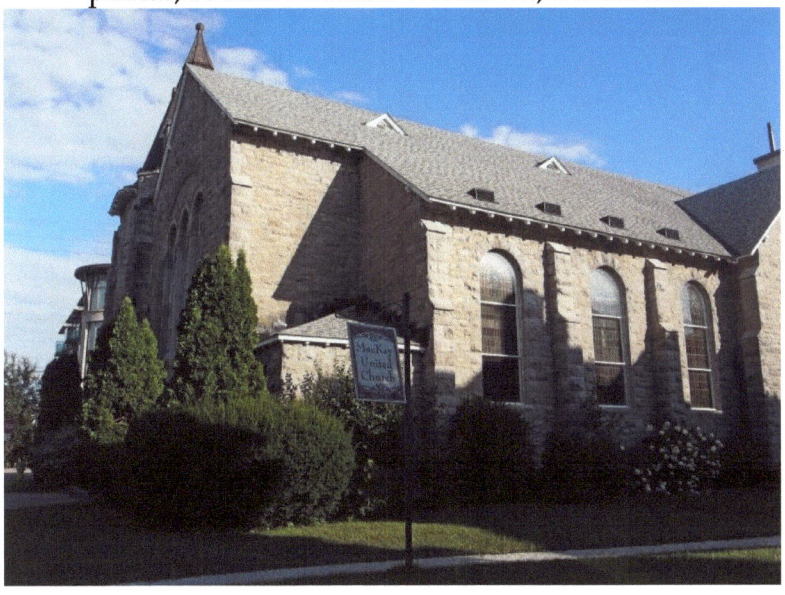

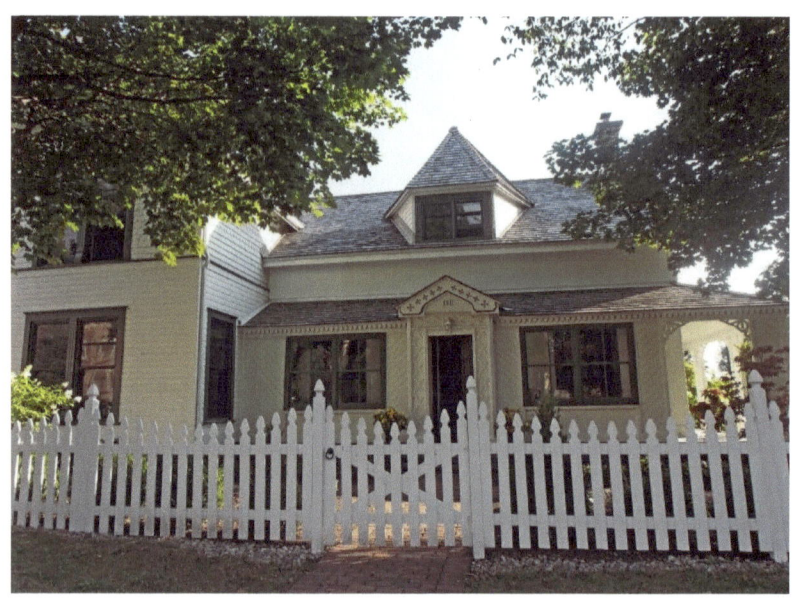

151 Stanley Avenue – dormer in attic

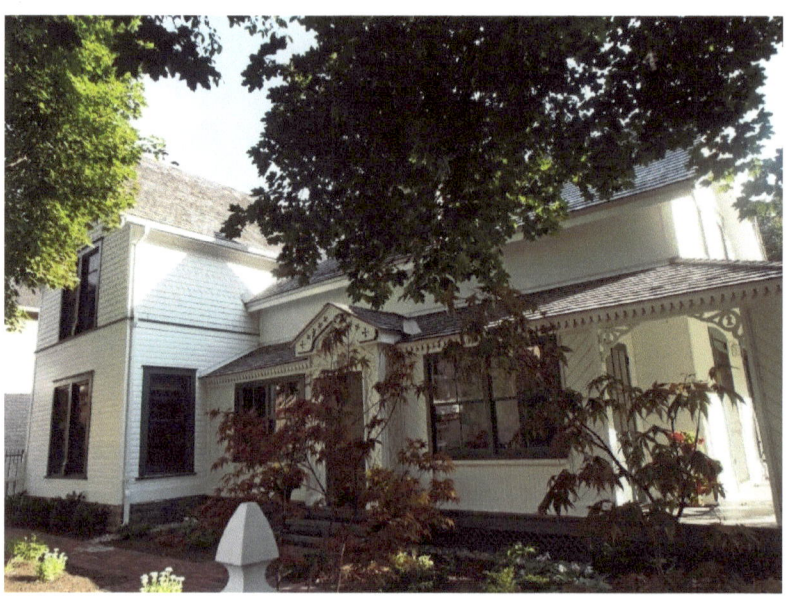

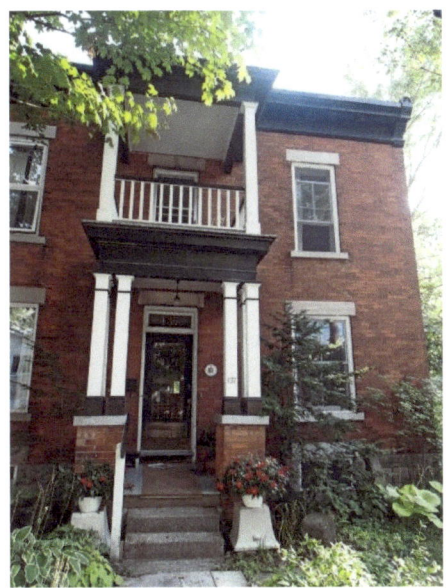

137 Stanley Avenue

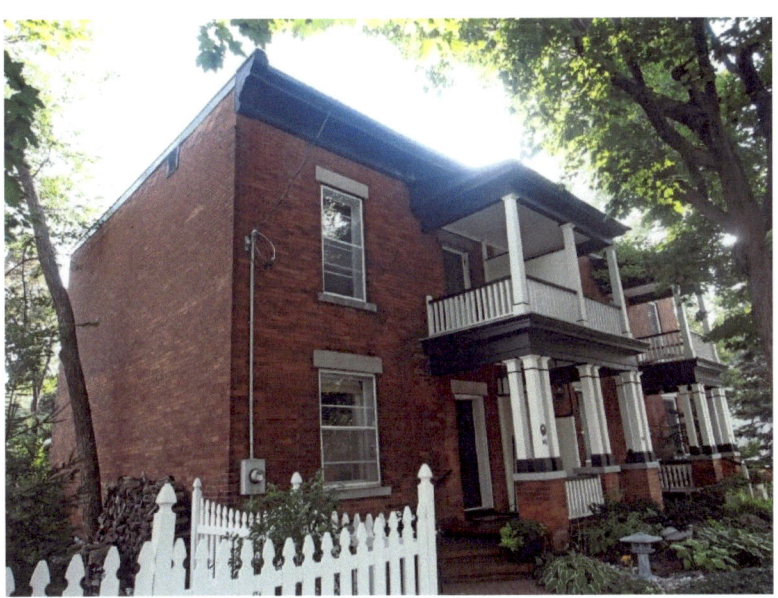

137-141 Stanley Avenue – second floor balconies

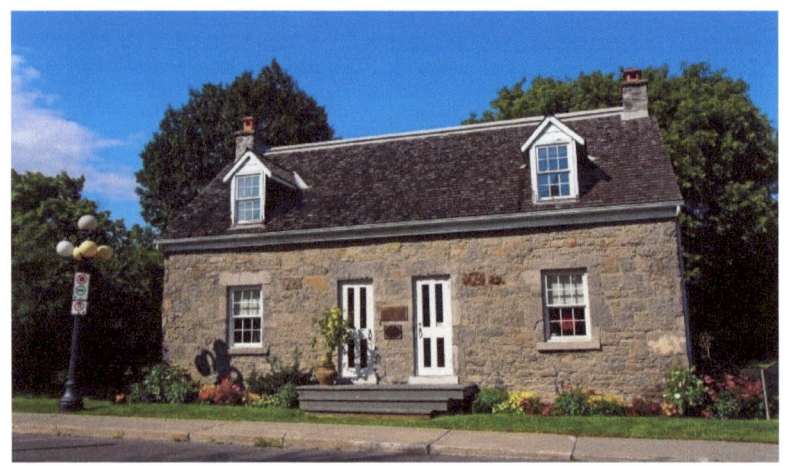

62 John Street – The Frazer Schoolhouse was built c. 1837 by
Thomas Mackay, the founder of New Edinburgh. Between
1838 and 1843, it served as New Edinburgh's first school.
James Fraser lived in one side and taught the children in the
other. It reverted to a double residence in 1844.
Dormers

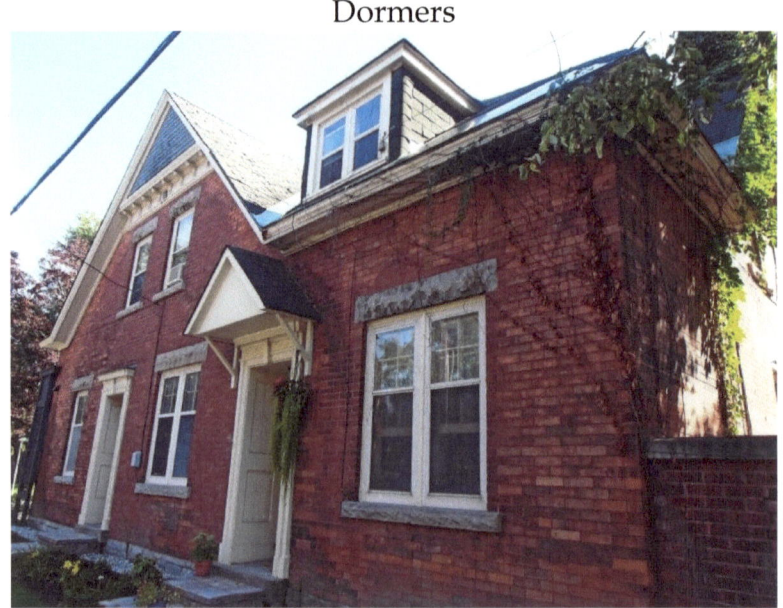

83-85 John Street – brackets on gable, dormer

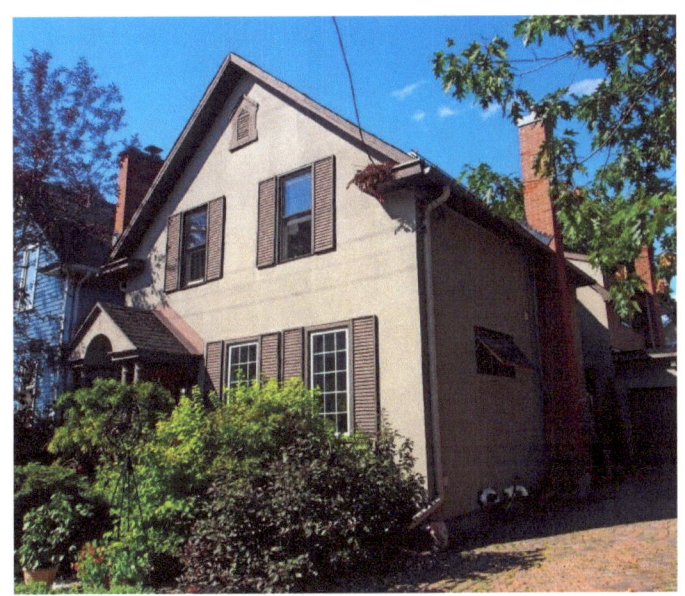

Cornice return on gable

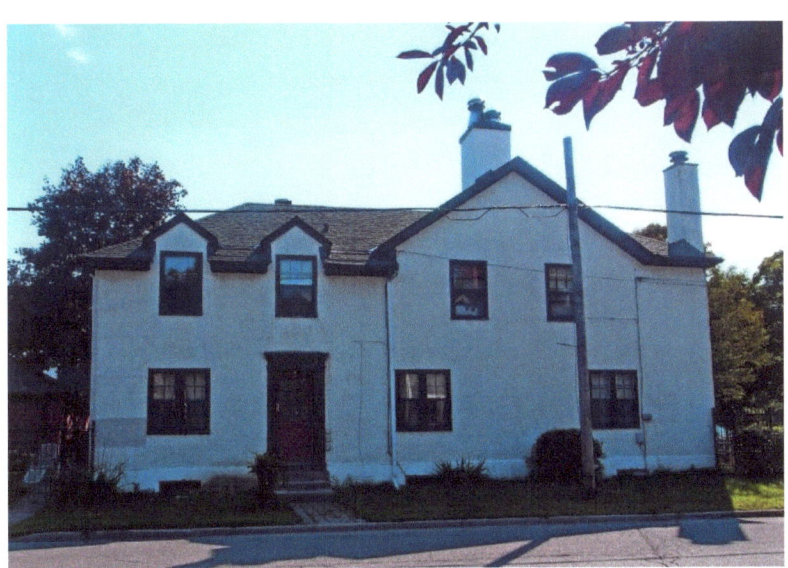

John Street

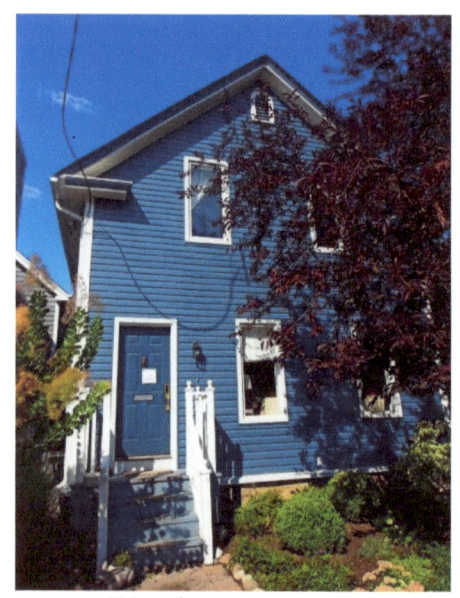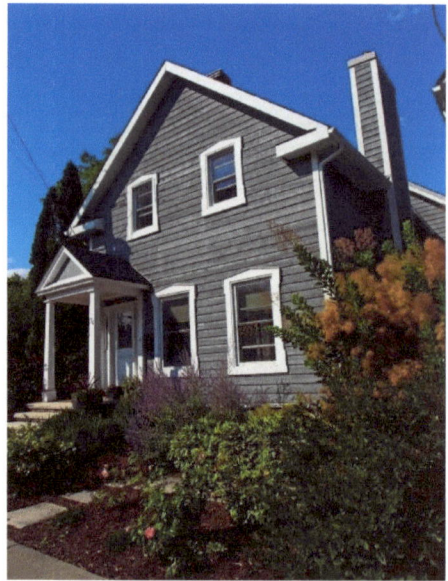

76 John Street   74 John Street

Cornice return on gables – Victorian style

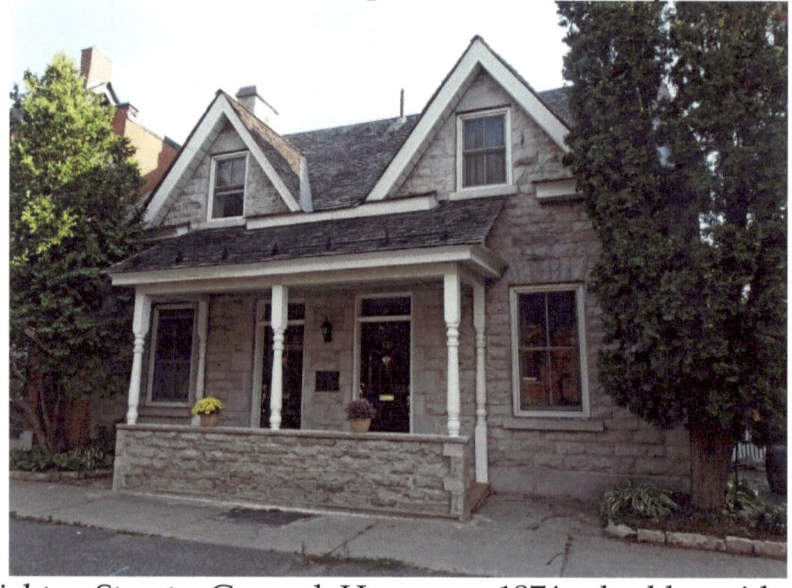

Crichton Street – Garvock House – c. 1874 - double residence
built by Alexander Garvock, a stone mason

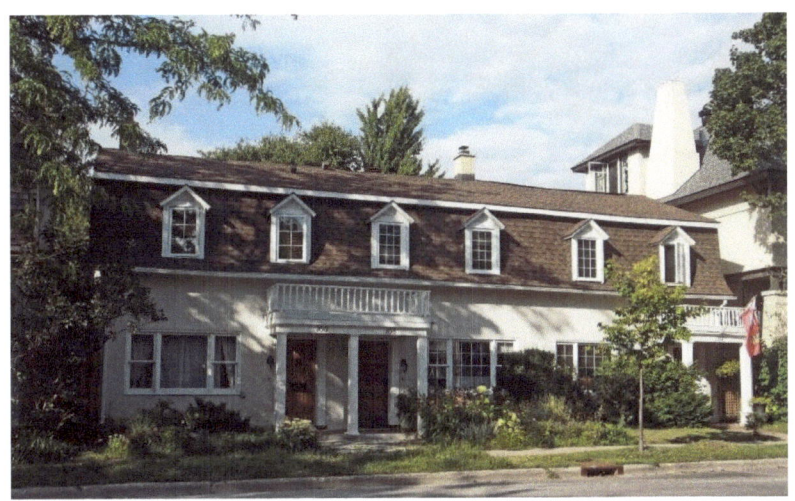

166-170 Crichton Street

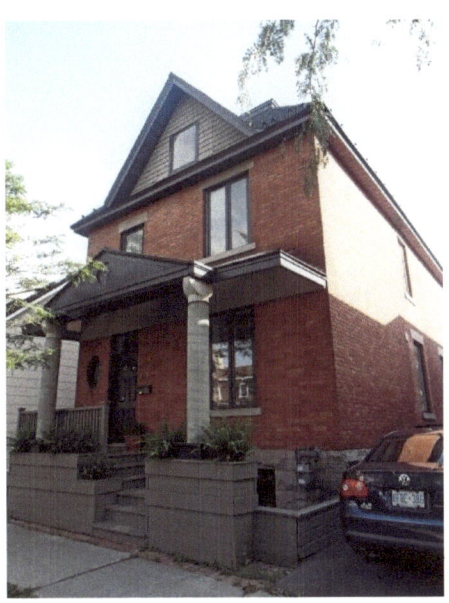

165 Crichton Street

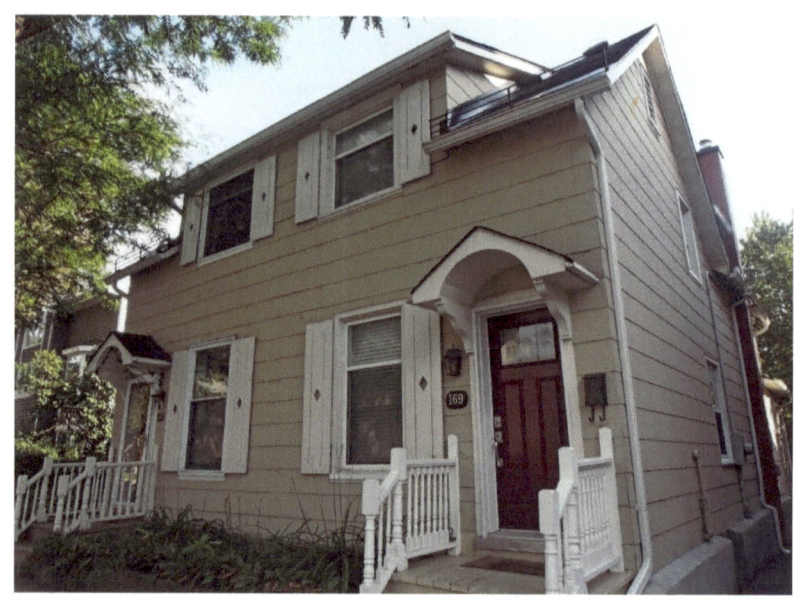

169-171 Crichton Street

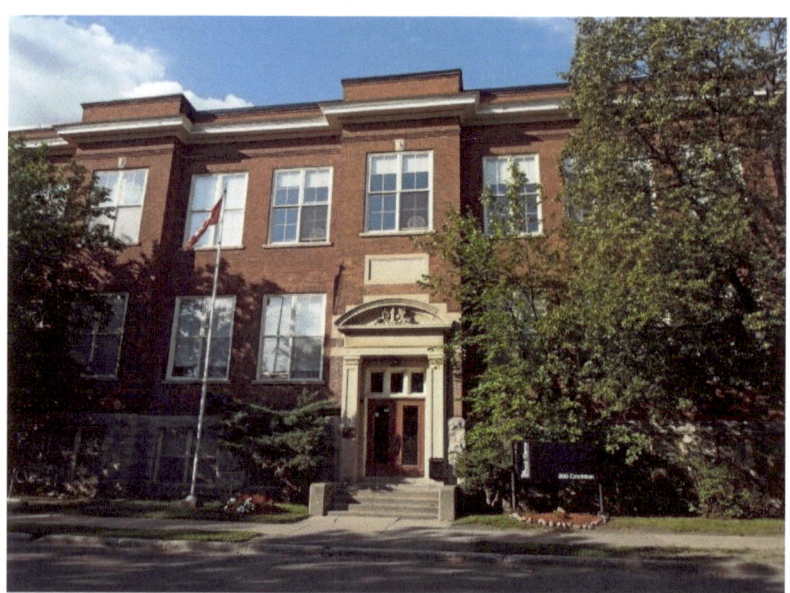

200 Crichton Street – Crichton Street Public School – 1919 – pediment above door with decorated tympanum, dentil molding below pediment

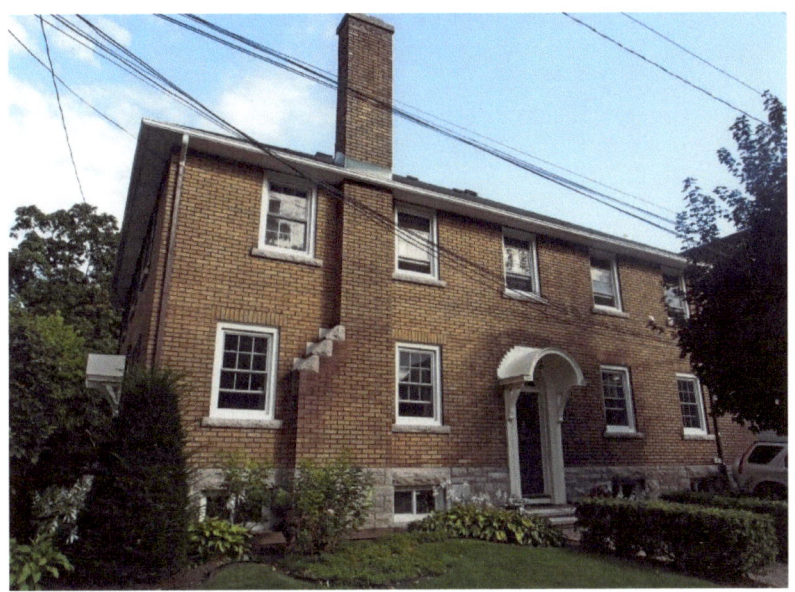

Keefer Street – Georgian style

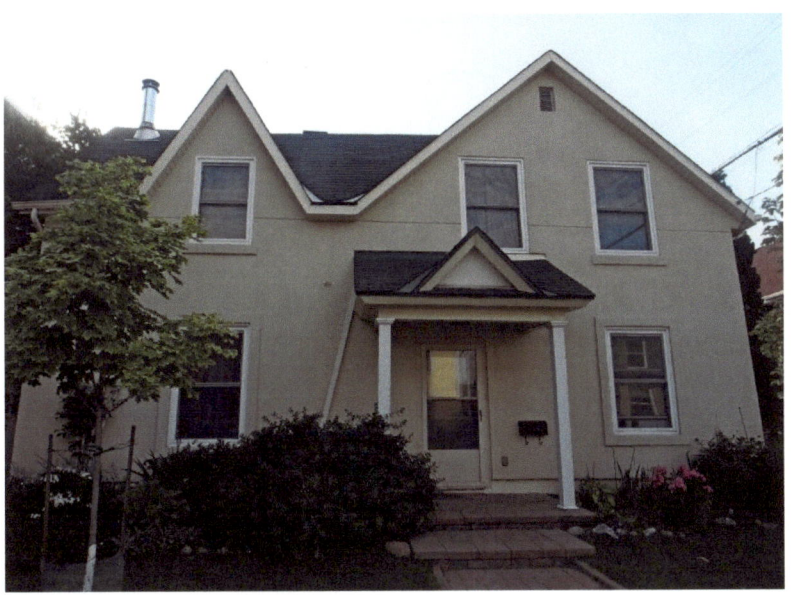

Keefer Street - Victorian

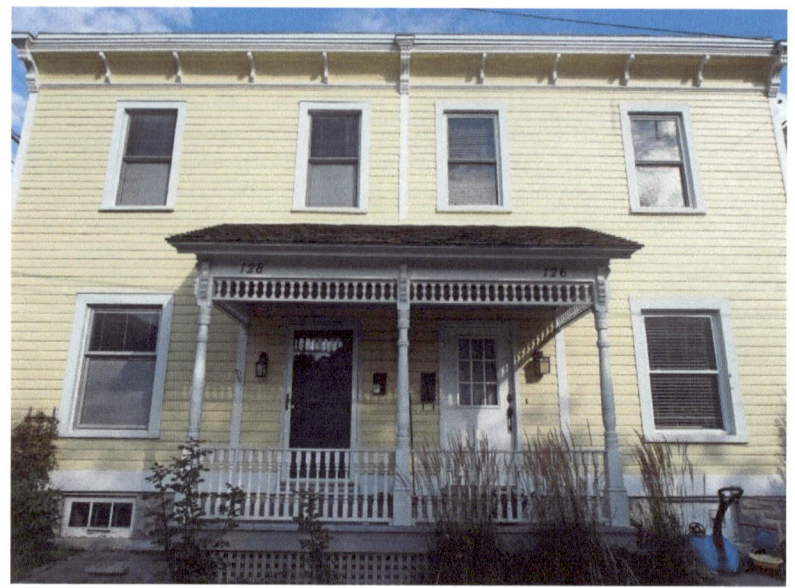

126-128 Keefer Street - wood-turned decorative support posts
and open railing

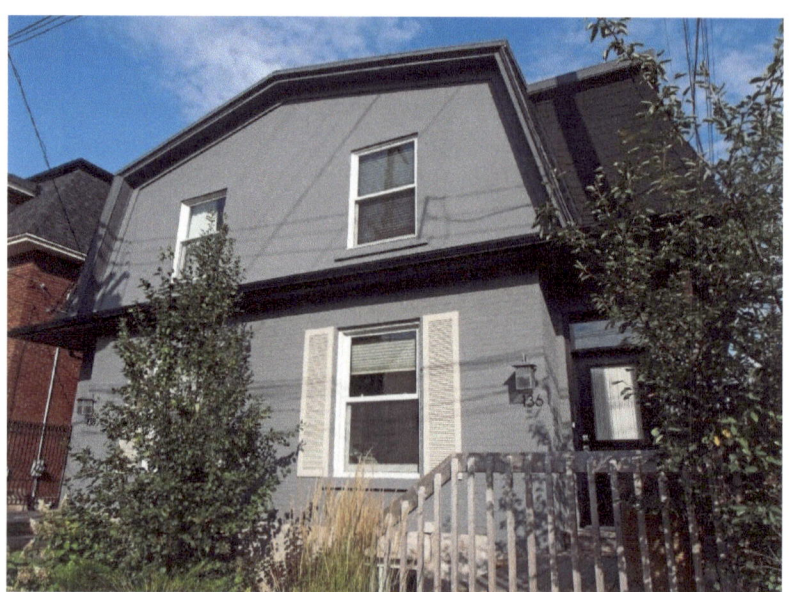

136 Keefer Street – gambrel roof

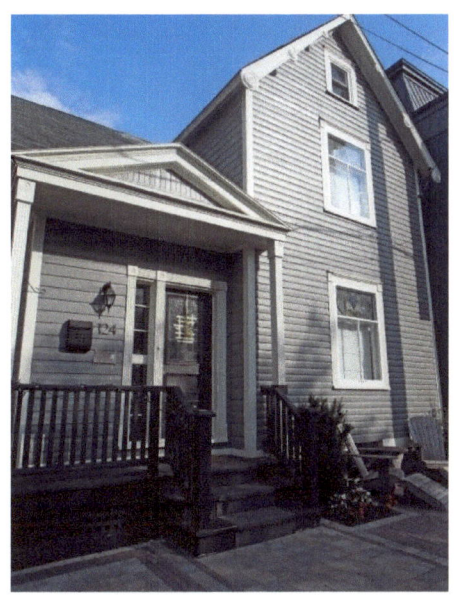

Keefer Street - pediment

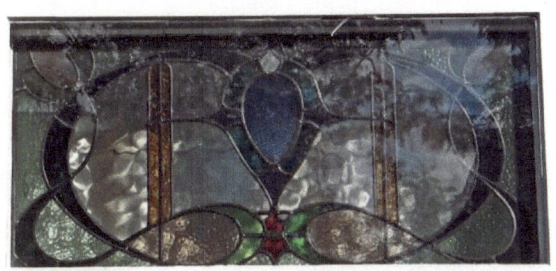

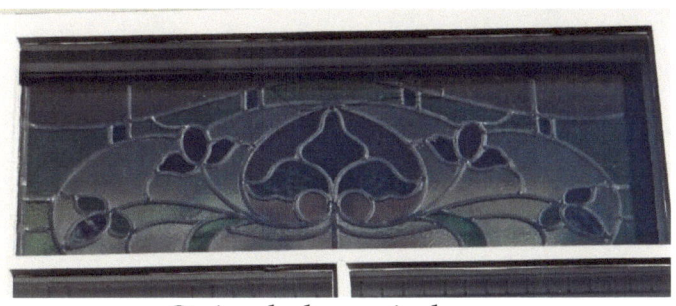

Stained glass windows

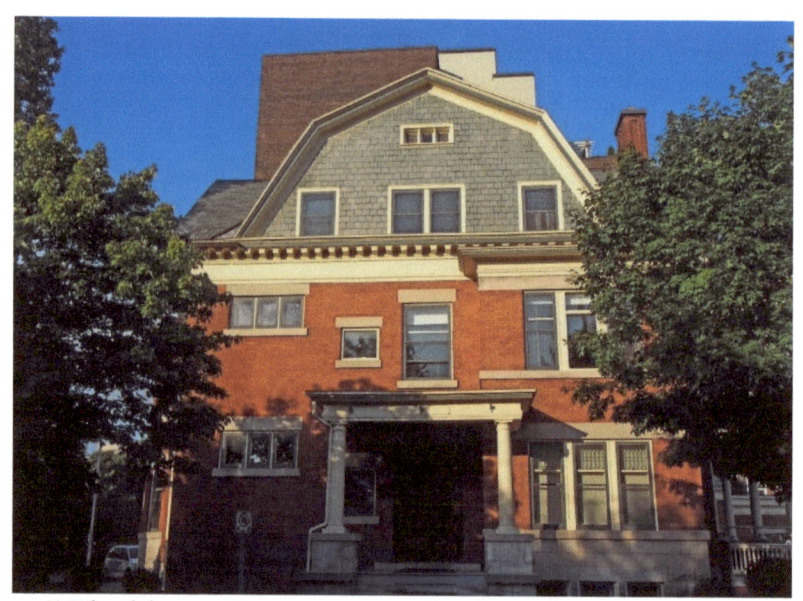

5 Blackburn Avenue – gambrel roof – Cape Dutch
architecture, Doric pillars

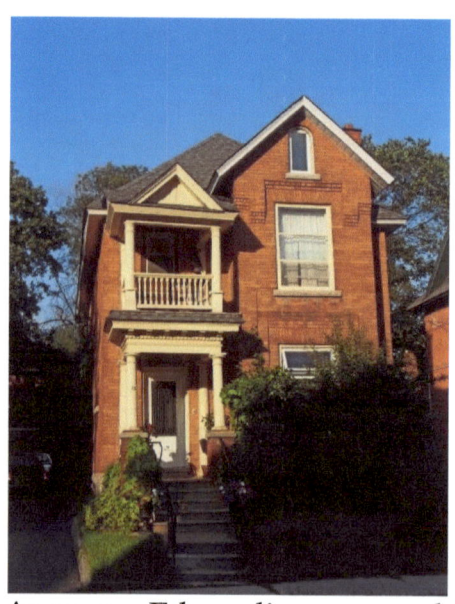

15 Blackburn Avenue – Edwardian – second floor sleeping
porch with pediment above

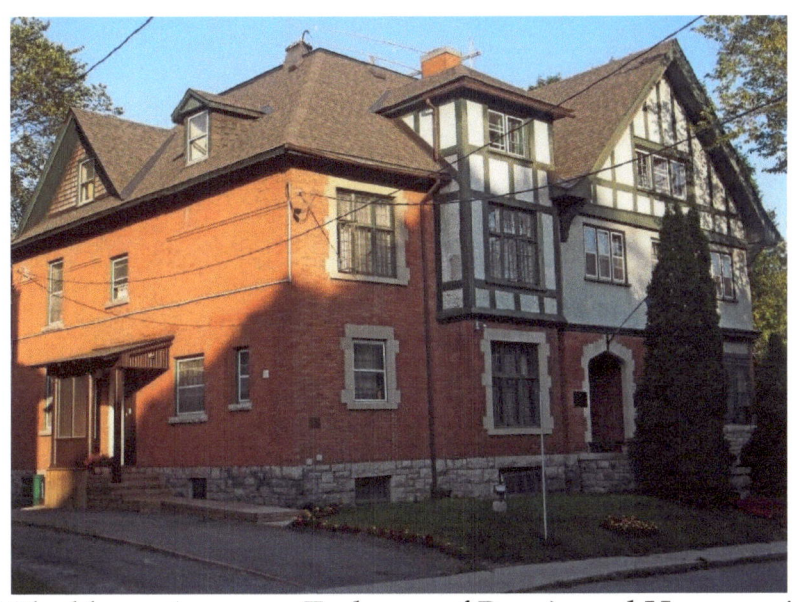

17 Blackburn Avenue - Embassy of Bosnia and Herzegovina
– Tudor style – half-timbering, dormers

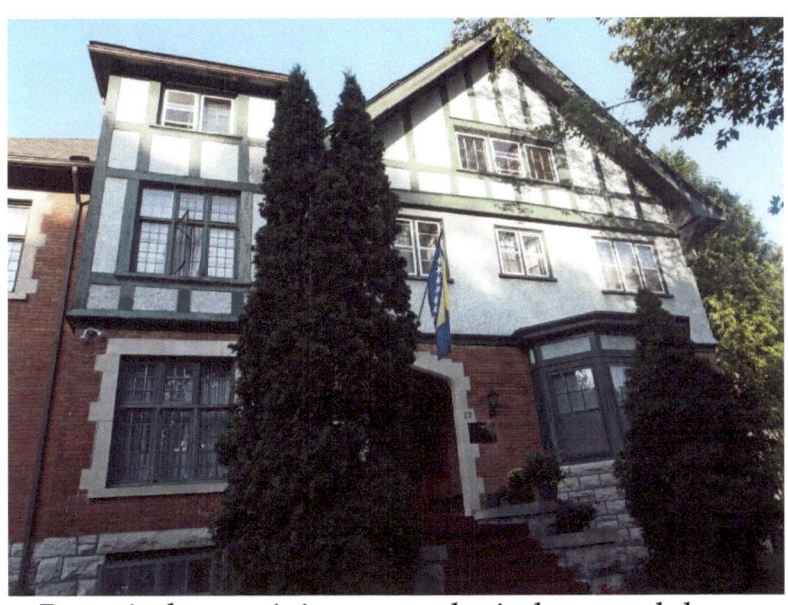

Bay window, qoining around windows and doors

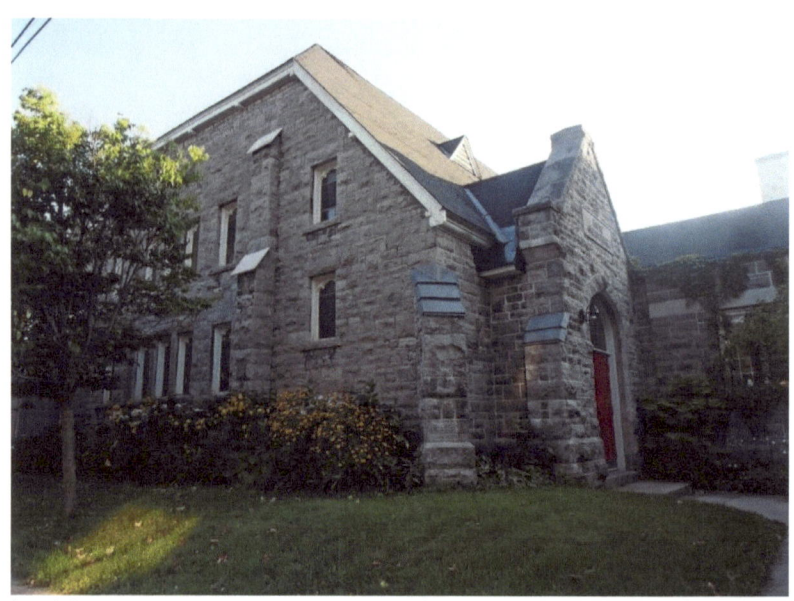

10 Blackburn Avenue - Sandy Hill's All Saints church re-made into community hub - Bate Memorial Hall will be torn down to make way for new ground-floor businesses, several floors of offices and several more above that for condos.

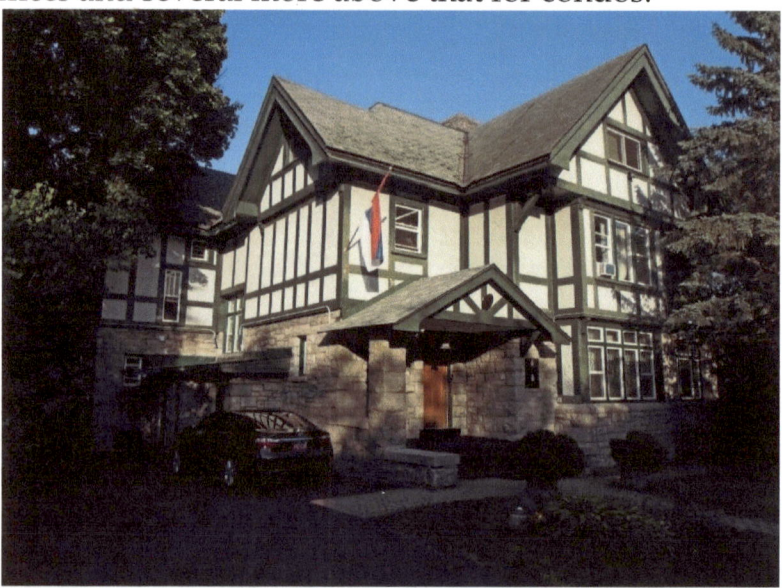

Blackburn Avenue - Tudor – half-timbering, pediment

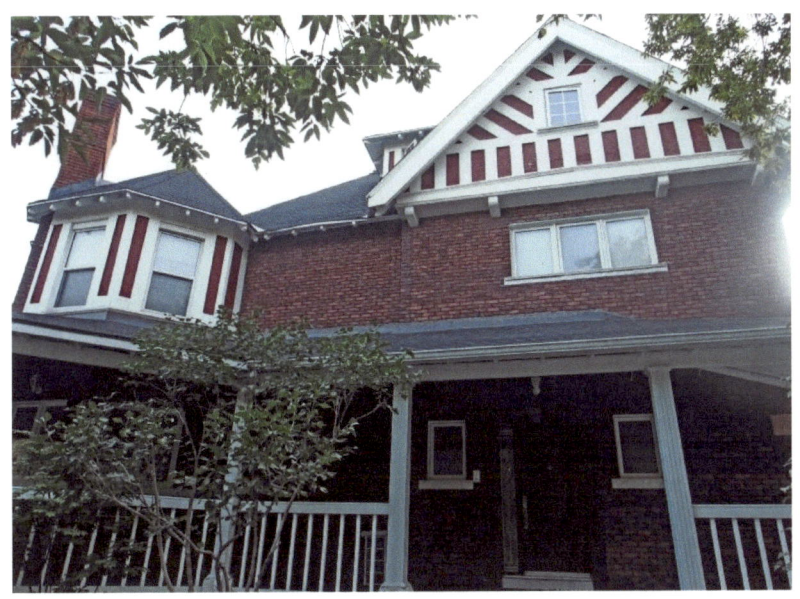

Blackburn Avenue – red and white decorative gable

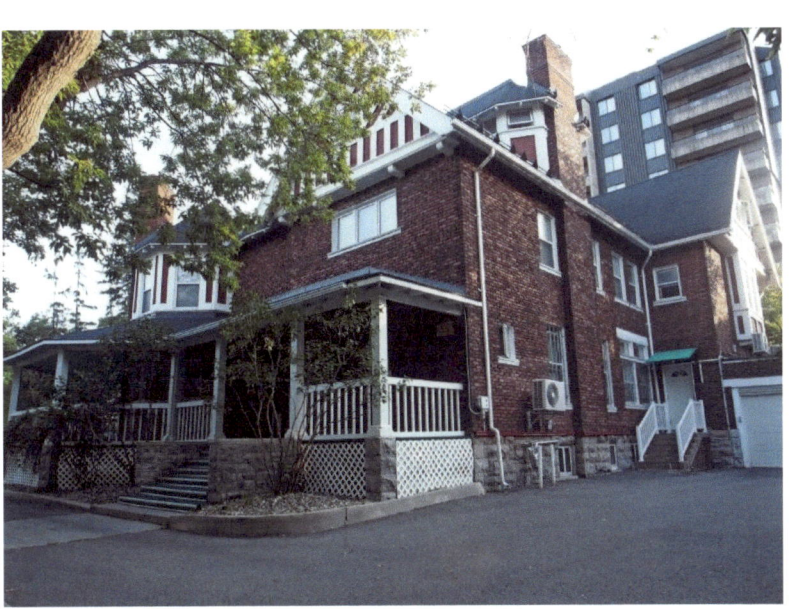

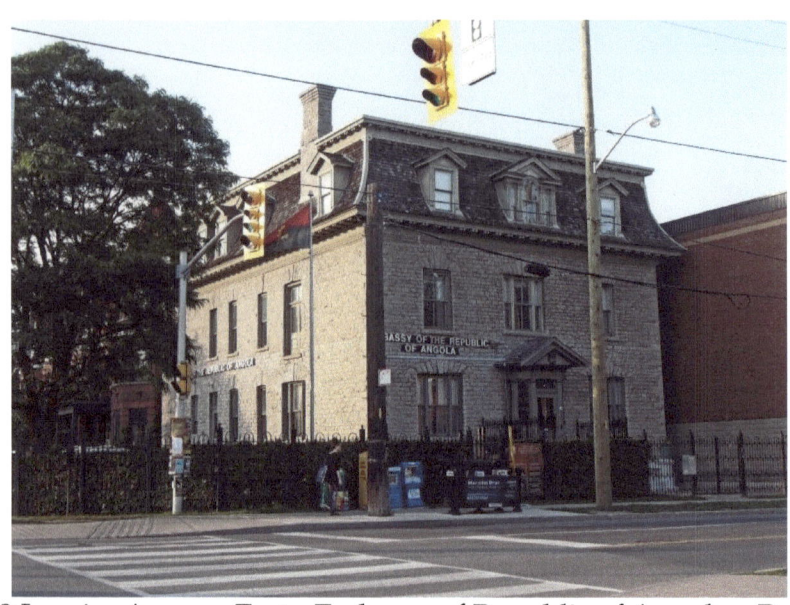

189 Laurier Avenue East - Embassy of Republic of Angola – Panet House – built in 1876 - Second Empire style – mansard roof, dormers

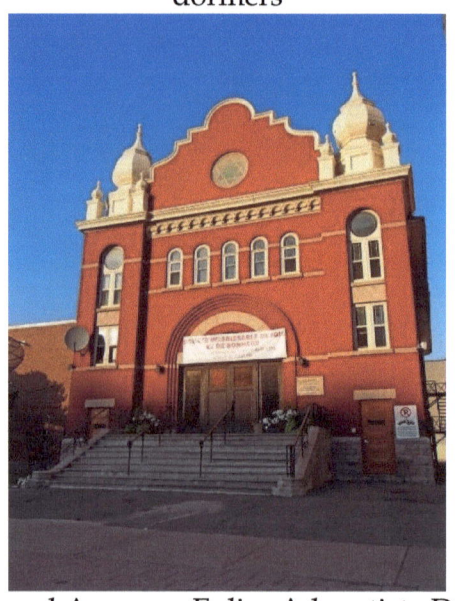

375 King Edward Avenue - Eglise Adventiste Du 7 ième Jour Francophone D'Ottawa – domes, Jacobean gable, decorative cornice

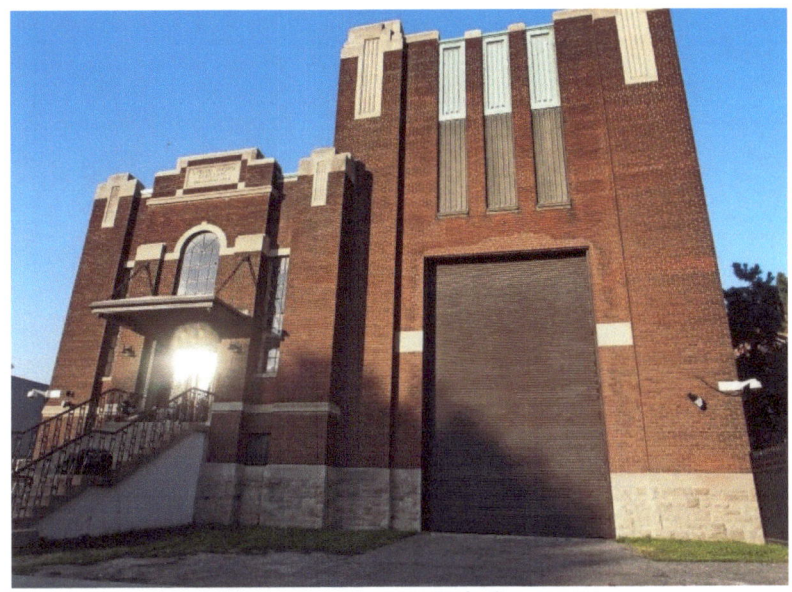

Ottawa Hydro Electric Sub-Station No. 4

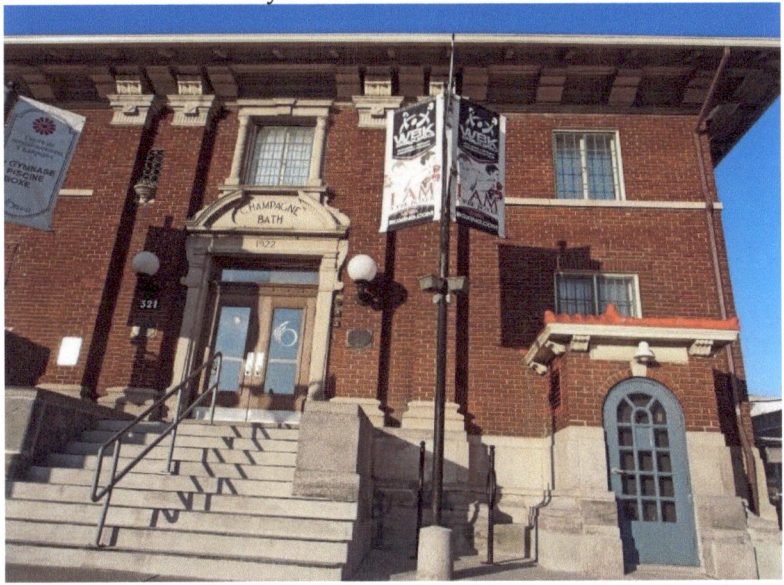

321 King Edward Avenue - Champagne Bath – 1922 – a blend of Spanish Colonial Revival and Prairie styles - named after Ottawa mayor Napoleon Champagne - it was Ottawa's first municipal swimming pool - it was salt water - originally the structure was built for the greater hygiene of the largely working class residents of the neighborhood, many of whom had no baths in their homes.

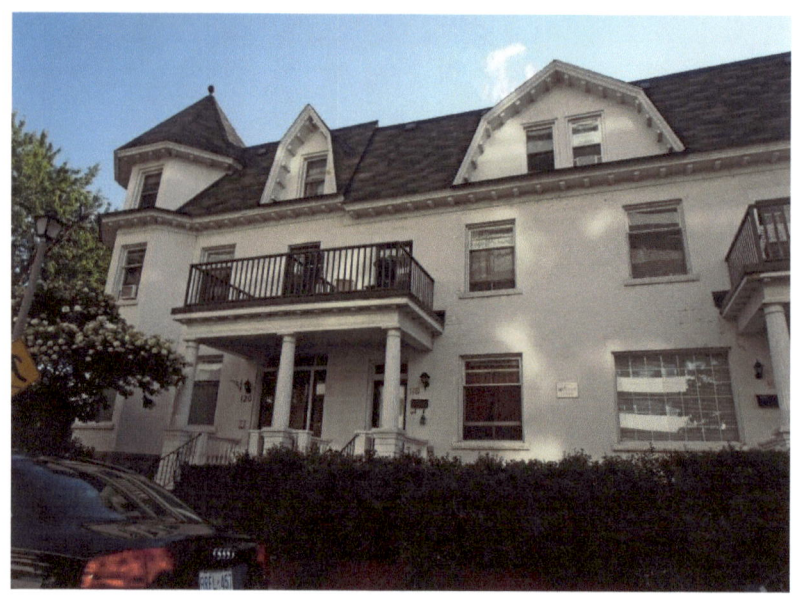

114-120 Wurtemburg Street – corner turret, gambrel gables,
Doric capitals for porch supports with balcony above

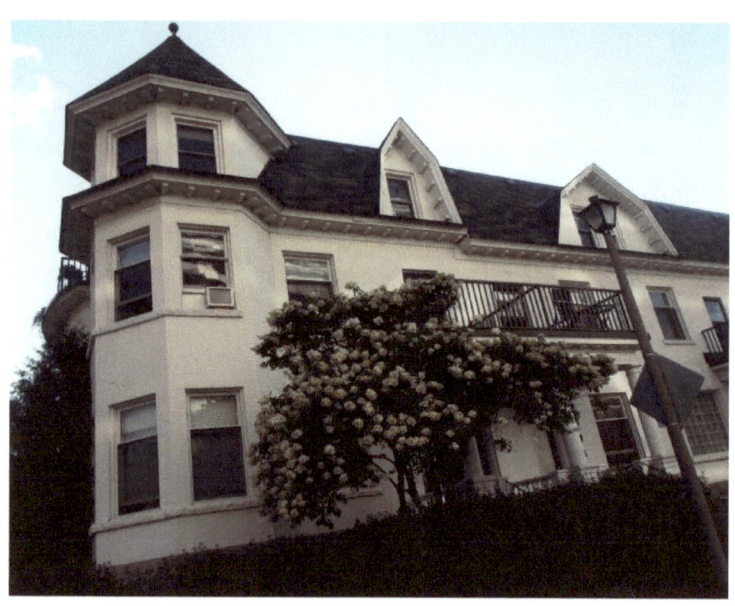

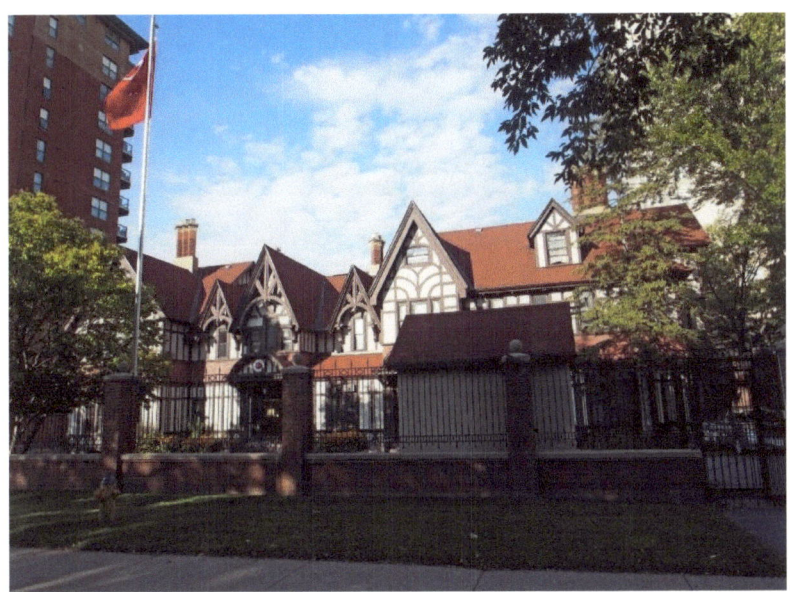

197 Wurtemburg Street – 1869 - Embassy of the Republic of Turkey - Tudor style – The central portion of the building was a picturesque Gothic Revival structure constructed for W.F. Whitcher, Commissioner of Fisheries. The two wings and the Tudoresque half-timbering were added when the structure served as a Children's Hospital from 1888-1904.

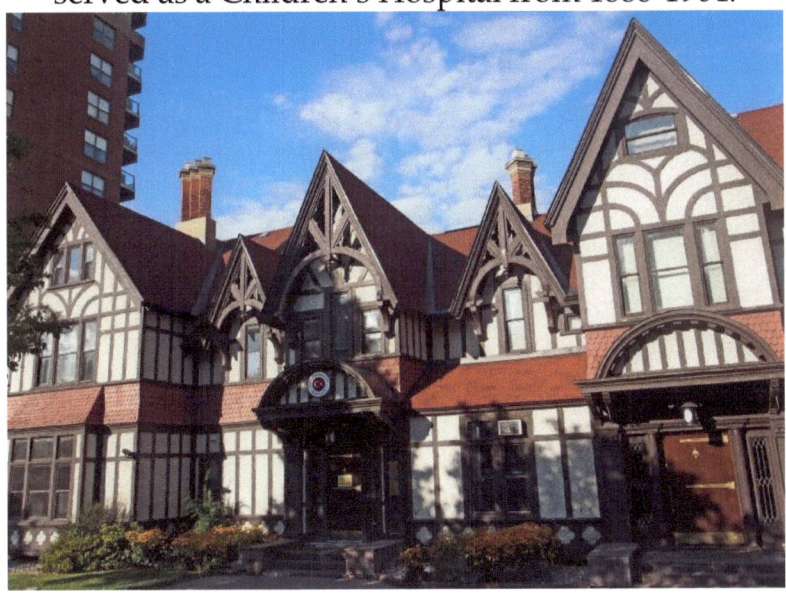

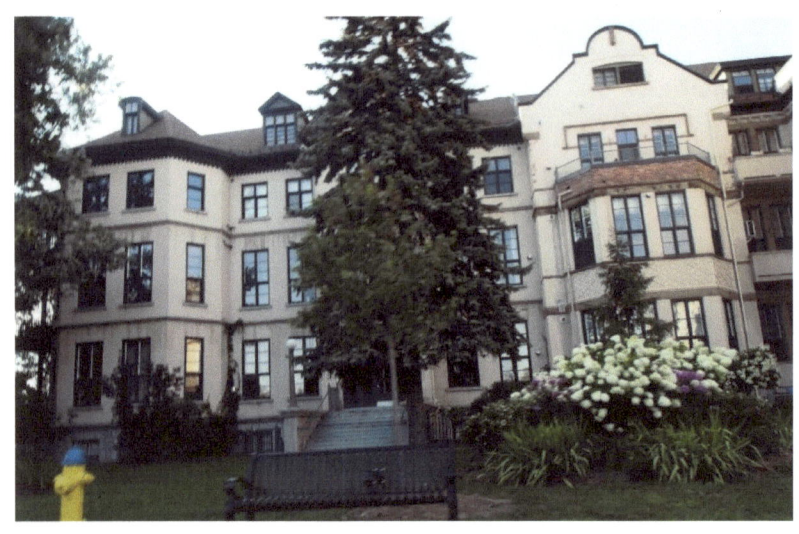

Wurtemburg Street - dormers, two-storey bay window with balcony off third floor and topped by a Jacobean gable

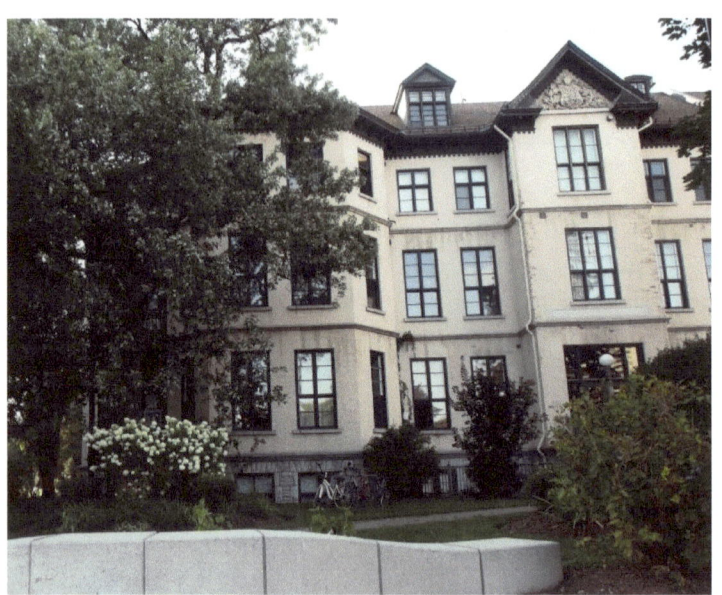

Cornice return on gable with crest

Architectural Terms

Banding: Different materials, colors or textures used in horizontal bands along a wall. Example: 81 Mackay Street, Page 28	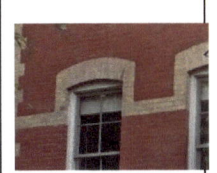
Bay Window: A window that projects out from a wall, in a semicircular, rectangular, or polygonal design. Used frequently in Gothic and Victorian designs. Example: 73 Mackay Street, Page 28	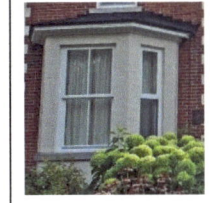
Buttress: a masonry structure built against or projecting from a wall which serves to support or reinforce the wall. In Canadian architecture, they are sometimes used for decoration. Example: 125 Mackay Street	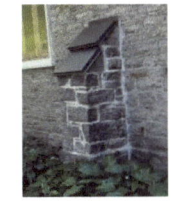
Capital: The uppermost finish or decoration on a column. A Doric column is characterized by a plain column with no base, a shaft with twenty flutings, and a simple capital with a simple entablature. Example: 5 Blackburn Avenue, Page 46	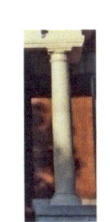
Cornice: originally the wooden overhang of the roof. With the use of stone, brick, iron and steel, the cornice is any projecting shelf at the top of a ceiling or roof. They can be very decorative. Example: 375 King Edward Avenue, Page 50	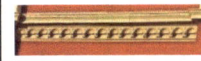

Cornice Return: decorative element on the end of a gable. Example: 255 Mackay Street, Page 33	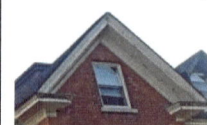
Cupola: A domed or curved roof rising from a building as a decorative element. Example: 528 Old St. Patrick Street, Page 34	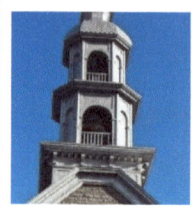
Dentil Moulding: an even series of rectangles used as ornamental decoration in cornices. Example: 200 Crichton Street, Page 42	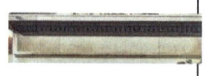
Dome: Any roof structure that is curved and spans a circular base. Example: 375 King Edward Avenue, Page 50	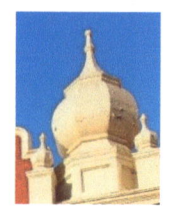
Dormer: (French for "sleep") a gable end window that pierces through the plane of a sloping roof surface to create usable space in the top floor or attic of a building by adding headroom. Example: 163 Mackay Street, Page 30	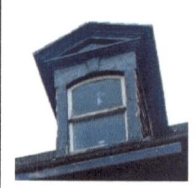

Gable: the triangular portion of a wall between the edges of a sloping roof. **Jacobean Gable:** the gable extends above the roofline. Example: 375 King Edward Avenue, Page 50	
Gambrel Roof: a symmetrical two-sided roof with two slopes on each side; the upper slope is positioned at a shallow angle, while the lower slope is steep. It is similar to a mansard roof, but a gambrel has vertical gable ends instead of being hipped at the four corners of the building. Example: 5 Blackburn Avenue, Page 46	
Iron Cresting: A decorative ornament along the top of a roof. Iron cresting was popular in the Baroque era and also in Italianate, Victorian, Second Empire and Queen Anne styles of architecture. Example: 125 Mackay Street, Page 30	
Keystone: is the central stone that locks all the stones into position, allowing the arch to bear weight. A keystone is often enlarged and embellished. Example: 10 Sussex Drive, Page 25	
Mansard Roof: This style was popularized by Francois Mansart (1598-1666), an architect of the French Baroque period and fashionable during the Second French Empire (1852-1870). This roof is almost flat on the top section, with two slopes on each of its sides with the lower slope at a steeper angle than the upper and having dormer windows. Example: 189 Laurier Avenue East, Page 50	

Pediment: a triangular section above the horizontal structure (entablature), typically supported by columns. The inside of the triangle is called the tympanum. Example: 81 Mackay Street, Page 28	
Pilaster: a slightly projecting column built into or applied to the face of a wall for additional structural support. Example: 1 Sussex Drive, Page 7	
Quoin: masonry blocks at the corner of a wall, often a decorative feature, usually larger or of a different colour than the rest of the wall. Example: 73 Mackay Street, Page 28	
Sidelight: a window, usually with a vertical emphasis, that flanks a door, and is often used to emphasize the importance of a primary entrance. **Transom Window:** the light above the doorway, also called a fanlight. Example: House on Page 26	
Verge board and Finial: also called bargeboards – hang from the projecting end of a roof and are often elaborately carved and ornamented. **Finial:** ornament added to the top of a gable, pinnacle, canopy or spire – a Gothic element. Example: 73 Mackay Street, Page 28	

Building Styles

Cape Dutch architecture is a traditional Afrikaner architectural style found mostly in the Western Cape of South Africa. The initial settlers of the Cape were primarily Dutch. When the Dutch came to Ontario, they brought with them building concepts from their own native lands. Architecture from the 18th and early 19th centuries in Ontario includes a wide assortment of detailing and ornament all applied to a basic building design centred around the fireplace and the source of water. Example: 5 Blackburn Avenue, Page 46	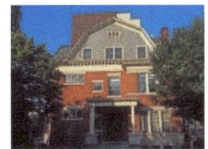
Classical Revival (1820 - 1860) – This style was an analytical, scientific, and dogmatic revival based on intensive studies of Greek and Roman buildings, concerned with the application of Greek plans and proportions to civic buildings. Schools, libraries, government offices, and most other civic buildings were built in the Classical Revival style. The white columned porches of the Classical Revival domestic buildings are identified with the mansions of wealthy land owners in Canada. Example: 35 Mackay Street, Page 27	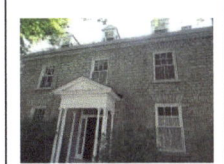
Edwardian, 1900-1930 – This style bridges the ornate and elaborate styles of the Victorian era and the simplified styles of the 20th century. Balanced facades, simple roof lines, dormer windows, large front porches, and smooth brick surfaces are its characteristics. Example: 15 Blackburn Avenue, Page 46	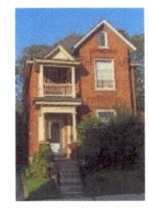

Georgian, before 1860 – This style began with the British King Georges in the 18th century. These buildings have balanced facades around a central door, medium-pitched gable roofs, and small paned windows. Late Georgian style is also called Regency architecture. Example: Rideau Hall, Page 7	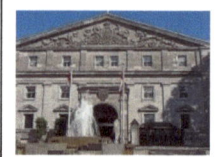
Gothic Revival, 1830-1890 – These decorative buildings have sharply-pitched gables with highly detailed verge boards, pointed-arch window openings, and dichromatic brickwork. It is a common style in Ontario. Example: 73 Mackay Street, Page 28	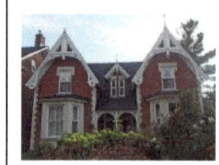
Neocolonial (also Colonial Revival, Georgian Revival or Neo-Georgian) architecture seeks to revive elements of architectural style of American colonial architecture of the period around the Revolutionary War which drew strongly from Georgian architecture of Great Britain. Architecture from the 18th and early 19th centuries in Ontario includes a wide assortment of detailing and ornament applied to a design centered around the fireplace and the source of water. Structures are typically two stories, have a symmetrical front facade with elaborate front doorways, often with decorative crown pediments, fanlights, and sidelights, symmetrical windows flanking the front entrance, often in pairs or threes, and columned porches. Example: 187 Mackay Street, Page 32	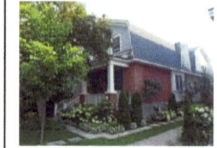

Prairie style, 1900-1940 - is one of the only purely North American styles. The horizontal lines, projecting eaves and geometric patterning of finishes and windows contrast sharply with the more formal, Classical styles taken from ancient Greece. Vernacular materials, stone, brick, and natural wood were preferred for finishes and often stained glass with patterns taken from nature were added. Prairie buildings are generally domestic and have a geometric patterning that is immediately evident. The complete lack of historicizing detail is deliberate and points to the trends found later in the century. Example: 321 King Edward Avenue, Page 51	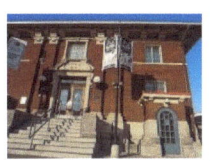
Regency Cottage, 1830-1860 – This style originated in England in 1815 and spread to Ontario later in the 19th century as British officers retired to Canada. It is a modest one-storey house with a low-pitched hip roof and has a symmetrical front façade. Example: 123 Mackay Street, Page 29	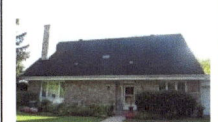
Tudor Revival – exposed timbers with stucco infill, multi-paned windows. Example: 197 Wurtemburg Street, Page 53	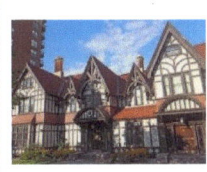

Renaissance Revival (1870 - 1910) - The Renaissance Palazzo was a three or four storey building with a rusticated (very large masonry blocks with deep joints and decorated with rough or bold finishes) ground floor, and regularized understated windows on two upper levels, always finished by an elaborate cornice. In Ontario, the Renaissance was revived in commercial buildings, banks, offices, and churches in many towns. Most of the Renaissance Revival buildings are designed without columns while those with columns and pilasters are more ornate. Example: 1 Sussex Drive, Page 7	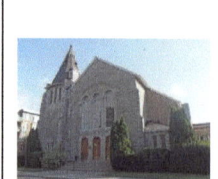
Romanesque Revival, 1880-1910 – This style hearkens back to medieval architecture of the 11th and 12th centuries with a heavy appearance, blocky towers and rounded arches. Example: 39 Dufferin, Page 35	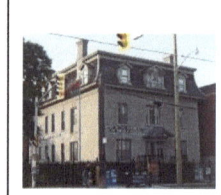
Second Empire, 1860-1880 – The mansard roof is the most noteworthy feature of this style and is evidence of the French origins. Projecting central towers and one or two-storey bays can also be present. Example: 189 Laurier Avenue East, Page 50	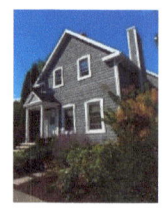
Victorian - In Ontario, a Victorian style building can be seen as any building built between 1840 and 1900 that doesn't fit into any of the other categories. It encompasses a large group of buildings constructed in brick, stone, and timber, using an eclectic mixture of Classical and Gothic motifs. Example: 74 John Street, Page 40	

www.ingramcontent.com/pod-product-compliance
Lightning Source LLC
Chambersburg PA
CBHW040848180526
45159CB00001B/351